GW01367259

Furnishing the Details

GMIT at Letterfrack

exhibition catalogue

Furnishing the Details is a joint exhibition venture between Farmleigh Gallery and GMIT at Letterfrack, hosted at Farmleigh Gallery from October 5th to November 5th, 2006.

GMIT would like to acknowledge the support of Minister Éamon Ó Cuív, T.D., and the Department of Community, Rural & Gaeltacht Affairs

FOREWORD

The Galway-Mayo Institute of Technology (GMIT) is a multi-campus third level Institute catering for 4500 full time and 4500 part time students. Its four campuses at Galway (Dublin Road and Cluain Mhuire), Castlebar and Letterfrack provide for education and research through a variety of disciplines.

GMIT programmes in Letterfrack are run in partnership with Connemara West - a community and rural development organisation based in North-West Connemara. Since 1987, the partnership has run furniture courses in Letterfrack.

The aim of GMIT at Letterfrack is to provide a dynamic educational environment to support students on a path of development towards creativity and expertise in furniture and wood based technologies.

Letterfrack is synonymous in the mind of the average Irish person with being a centre of excellence in furniture design, making, restoration and production and in this it is unique in Irish third level education. Currently there are six Bachelor of Science degrees on offer in Letterfrack.

Our programmes are most in demand from the Leaving Certificate student body. We actively encourage students from abroad and we have formal educational links with colleges and universities in Spain, Germany, Finland, the Czech Republic and the United States. Mature students and lifelong learners from at home and abroad are also very welcome on our programmes.

The aim of this exhibition at Farmleigh Gallery is to display and highlight the essence, excellence and variances of the programmes in GMIT Letterfrack in a highly professional, striking and visually exciting manner which is informative and interesting to all viewers.

Furnishing the Details will focus on excellence and innovation in contemporary furniture design; excellence in making; restoration; production; research and technology.

Management at GMIT and Letterfrack recognise and acknowledge the excellent promotional opportunity this exhibition affords the Institute in showcasing its work at Letterfrack to a national audience. The exhibition is a joint venture between the management of Farmleigh Gallery and the Letterfrack campus. I would like to acknowledge the help and support received from Mary Heffernan and Catherine Giltrap of Farmleigh and as Farmleigh is an OPW managed heritage property, I would like to acknowledge the assistance of the Office of Public Works. My thanks also to Paul Austen, Anthony Clare and Maria Sheridan from the Letterfrack exhibition committee.

GMIT at Letterfrack would like to thank all of the students (past and present) who have lent works for this exhibition; the Department of Community, Rural and Gaeltacht Affairs, the title sponsor of this show. Our partner sponsors: GMIT and Connemara West. Finally, we would like to extend thanks to Anne Brady and Conor O'Riordan for designing the catalogue, Mary O'Malley for her essay, Jennifer Goff for the catalogue text and editorial assistance, and Joe Geoghegan for photography.

Michael Hannon, Head of Centre,
GMIT at Letterfrack.

REMARKS BY PRESIDENT MARY McALEESE ON VISITING GMIT LETTERFRACK ON THE 27th JUNE, 2006

On the 27th June 2006, we had the honour and pleasure of a visit to GMIT Letterfrack by President of Ireland, Mary McAleese. President McAleese officially opened the new Furniture Gallery in the Galway-Mayo Institute of Technology (GMIT) Letterfrack campus and viewed *Letterfrack 2006*, the end of year graduate exhibition of work by students in the GMIT Furniture College. The President also presented six students with awards and unveiled a wooden plaque to mark the opening of the new Gallery. The following text is an excerpt from the speech which she made on this memorable day in Letterfrack.

I am delighted to be in your company on this gorgeous day, a beautiful day to be here in Letterfrack, a day of particular sweetness for the students here. Congratulations first of all to those students who were rewarded for their excellence today by being acknowledged as the best of their peers, the best of their group.

I want to say a very big thank you to the Director for the invitation to be here. It means a lot for me to be here, for a number of reasons actually, but there is almost a coalition of forces here. In another life, long before I became President, I lectured in Criminal Law, Criminology and Penology and the name Letterfrack meant something very different to me in those days. It stood for a kind of failure. Actually, it stood for a failure of families, it stood for a failure of institutional imagination. It stood also in some ways for a failure of humanity itself, because so many young men whose lives were already blighted in many different ways, found their way to this place and found a place from which they couldn't escape when they were here, and couldn't escape from it in adulthood. And the experience for many of them was an experience that diminished, an experience that reduced them as human beings.

That was the temper of the times and how wonderful now, over the last years, to hear the name of Letterfrack used in a very, very different context. I love wood and I have a respect for those who work with wood. In recent times I go to events and someone will say "that piece was made by a young girl and she is a graduate of Letterfrack", or "that was made by a young boy who is a graduate of Letterfrack", and then over a period you begin to realise that the word

REMARKS BY PRESIDENT MARY McALEESE ON VISITING GMIT LETTERFRACK ON THE 27th JUNE, 2006 (contd)

Letterfrack now means something very different. It means excellence, it stands for something that is very profound, that has really a very recent providence in Ireland and that is the freeing of imagination, the freeing of our young people to be what they want, to do what they want, to get the very best of education, to marry their own genius and their own passion to the best of training and to see where it goes.

Where does it take you? It's taken each one of the students here as individuals, it has taken them as artists, as craftsmen and women out into our country, out into the world, everyone of them ambassadors with a new meaning for the name of Letterfrack. And also as ambassadors for this new Ireland, this Ireland where we are hungry to see the unrepressed, the unsuppressed imagination, to see where our harness to education takes us. Unfortunately there was a time when we thought that the suppression of the human person and the repression of the human person, the physical fitting of them into tight little boxes was the good deal. We did not see what that did to the human spirit, and here now, in and through these magnificent pieces of work, we now see what happens to the unrestrained imagination, the imagination that is encouraged, that is supported, that is revelled in. Now we know that it is important that we revel in the genius of our young people and that we tell them how good they are, and that we inspire them to believe how brilliant they can be and how important it is to create the places, the spaces, the help and the structures which allow all that genius that is inside of them to reveal itself.

It is a place frankly, if I hadn't gone through a girls convent school in the 1960s, I would be here in Letterfrack. This is where I would be. This is the place I would most want to be. It is unusual to find an Institute of this excellence, a third-level Institute of this level of excellence in a tiny community. That also means a lot to me because, before I became President, one of the passions I had was to bring third-level education to small communities in the belief that here was a place that they could flourish, and flourish with a very special kind of uniqueness and peculiarity that you wouldn't get in the more conventional urban setting. Here you have done it and you've done it magnificently.

To drive along the road now, a road that is very familiar and a road that we often used to travel on, to see now what the buildings and the new buildings around are saying, the confidence they are exuding and how they respect the place but most importantly, they respect the students and they respect the staff, they give them wonderful, wonderful places to work in. This is a place that is meant to open up the human person, not to close it down. And that just shouts from these walls now, with a passion, with a determination born of all of our experience, born of all our bitter experience - but also born now out of very different times in our country, times when we know our future lies in the opening up of hearts and minds, giving them their confidence, giving them their voice, saying "Go on, do your best, show us what you are capable of". Now we look and we see what they are capable of and, in this room, we marvel at their genius, we marvel too at the commitment of these young people. It is wonderful to witness young men and young

FURNISHING THE DETAILS

women committing themselves to this pursuit of excellence with such diligence and extraordinary intelligence. We thank them because these are the young people who make us so proud.

I visited an exhibition in Farmleigh of young Irish craftsmen and women, every craft imaginable being represented including the skilled men and women of Letterfrack. I was electrified to think that this is what the young of Ireland are capable of doing at this time in their lives. What will they be like in 10 years time, what will they be like in 20 years time?

The wonderful thing I hear about the students here too is how much the graduates love to come back to this place, how tied they feel to it, so passionate are they about their vocation, about their mission, that they are so generous in sharing their lives subsequently with the students here. Whether you are young Irish men and women, whether you come from around the world to compliment us by following the name of Letterfrack, and come to study here, it makes us feel very, very proud.

To the staff at GMIT at Letterfrack, can I also say well done to each and every one of you. The idea and the concept was a new one, a very new one and a few people may have wondered how it would go. Well it was going to go as well as the people who came here made it go and you have done a job of outstanding, outstanding success. It is a job that you deserve such credit for, you deserve such thanks for because the investment you make in every single one of these young men and women is an investment not just in them. It's an investment in their community and it's an investment in their countries. In particular it's a wonderful investment in our country. I hope you feel so fulfilled in your work and I hope the young people feel as fulfilled in their vocation as I feel very proud to be here this day, to see it and to feel it and to wish with all my heart that I was having a different birthday altogether and that I was sitting with an A-level result and contemplating a future as a student here.

Mary McAleese
President of Ireland

FURNISHING THE DETAILS

'…Yet there is dangerous loss,
hanging like an unpainted Angelus.
We are going to pay our last respects
to the blacksmith. He worked

with definite tools, the hammer
the anvil and the tongs. They rang like bells
and sparks flew everywhere
from the hooves of newly shod horses

striking the road. They bellowed
out of the coals and rose
from the hot white iron struck
on the anvil when the forge

was a crucible, furious with the energy
of things being made – useful, a solid grate,
beautiful, a Faberge gate. A child watched.
She did not touch. This was real work,

holy somehow. The memories blaze
and realise. I have been mourning
for three days not what is gone
but the shape of what is left.'

From *The Forge*

To transform a building, first let in light. To inform a mind, banish fear. Then plant an idea. No place in Ireland was more suited to such an experiment than the remote Quaker village of Letterfrack. Few places had known more fear, few places have such a particular light. It reflects against the hills, glancing off the lake and the sea, backlighting the houses and the stark Victorian lines of the old Industrial School. In Winter it is Gothic as the apparition of Kylemore Abbey, rising out of the lake a few miles away, a monument to a man's grief for a bride's premature death.

GMIT Letterfrack Furniture College allows the old pain its place, uses the buildings and classrooms, and the architects and builders have opened the old thick walls and joined them with the new classrooms and workshops and high ceilings where the light slants in. To change a building you re-order space. There is little sense now, walking through the Furniture College, seeing the beautiful finished tables and bureaux and lamps that will be on view in Farmleigh, but seeing just as interestingly the new wood, the half-made chair, the semi-formed roughness that will become an outdoor shower, whimsical as a Philip Treacy hat, and seeing the detailed sketches for a candy coloured table, there is no sense of anything other than interest and hard work. A sense that this is what a college should be, with European accents and broken English and the local accent that is crucial to the success and survival of this wonderful endeavour.

First, let me furnish a few details from a child's life in an equally isolated village, twenty odd miles from Letterfrack, along a wilder coast. We had no Quaker village, no exotic marvel like Kylemore Abbey.

'What will you do when you grow up?' Like children everywhere, we were often asked this stock question. 'Where will you go when you grow up – America or England?' might as well have been the question. All over Connemara in the fifties, sixties and, except for a brief stay of execution, in the seventies, in the eighties and much of the nineties doing and going were sister verbs. Here is a memory:

It is a Winter evening, bitter and grey. The silence is broken by the cries of children at play. My makeshift hurley, the rough edges hurting my hand, shudders against the finger bone when it strikes another stick, hurting all the way up the arm. There is a hoking underfoot for the ball, a push, the stick snakes between my feet and the ball is gone. It is pucked way down the pitch, which is short and full of rocks. The other players are my sister and brother. The game is confused; there is scant respect for rules, even when they are known.

'Goal!'
'Foul. You fouled. Wasn't that a foul Daddy?'
'It was not.'
'You shoved me. She shoved me.'
'I did not. You're a liar.'
'And you're a coward!'

The hurley is brandished, a weapon. There is adult intervention. I am seven years old.

Or a Summer evening, towards nightfall. Children at play. A real hurley, the ash smooth and beautifully hefted, an effortless extension of the hand. Not as sore when the sticks clashed, more a ringing up the arm, the life of the tree still evident in the timber, like Ulysses' oar. The connection between the ash and the game is ancient and sacred. The small ball, not a real sliotar, is curving towards my goal. I lift the hurl, intercept the ball, pick it up on the stick, hop it and give a long puck, out of danger. On one such an evening, in a field that has no rocks, though a small turlough fills every Winter from a central spot known as 'The Big Hole', it is getting late and the air has cooled. The sky is clear and darkening so that the deep blue line that will be visible up to midnight is gaining definition over the ruined coastguard station. The Slyne Head lighthouse scans the village like radar, picks up the blip of the ball as it speeds towards me. I raise the hurley, nervous of missing. There is a lightening in the air, a slowing down of the ball's trajectory.

Between me and it, another dimension opens. In this endless moment I discovered magic. And physics. The dimension of the present moment, which, the distinguished Czech immunologist and poet Miroslav Holub tells us, in his essay of that name, lasts three seconds. I was taken aback to read this, as I have always considered the present moment to be infinitely elastic. Battalions of angels could be flying within its boundaries, or radio waves from outer space.

This was the moment I understood the value of something well made and the tensile beauty of ash. I didn't know that then. I was young and not a particularly observant child. But passive knowledge is stored unbeknownst to us and this fact forms the basis of the delicate art of teaching. Instruction is another matter altogether.

FURNISHING THE DETAILS (contd)

The other material I was familiar with was metal. The little girl is my young self. She is a little older than the child with the hurley, pulled by the first dangerous tides of adolescence. She is addicted to the transformative, the ancient primeval pull of fire.

Winter or Summer, the door of the forge never closed and the fire inside was never quenched for long. This was where dirty bits of iron were changed and turned into lovely shiny objects, where she first learned the meaning of the word 'wrought'. She didn't know then, nor for a long time to come, that the word for the man who made boats, boatwright, came from the same stem.

Hurrying, she heard the bright clang of metal being struck on the anvil before she reached the forge, and sometimes the blue light of the welding rod flashed out like a lightening tree, shorting and sparking. This was not the same as the light of the sun. It was hard and dangerous as if real lightening had been captured and trapped in those thin grey rods. When it got out you could hear its wild sizzle.

She looked into the darkened forge, carefully as she had been taught, to avoid the direct glare. The smith was a short man. He wore a special apron to protect his clothes. It was black and shiny down the front, from the anvil and from the horses' hooves rubbing against the leather when he held them against him as he pulled out the old nails and took off their worn out shoes.

This was the best place. This was where ugly lumps of metal were changed by fire and made into tulips for candlesticks, beautiful gates and the many kinds of horseshoes that were displayed above the big door which rolled along on a track, opening almost the whole front of the forge to the daylight. Inside there were shadows and mysteries. She knew nothing about what was called the elemental then, only the tingle along her skin at the chaos and the fire and the bright loud sounds of metal striking metal. She watched the shapes emerging, her uncle holding a great square mask before his eyes. It was black and made of metal, with a tinted glass window that allowed him to see what he was doing. She had to look away while he was welding, though once he let her hold the mask, just to see what it was like, how to darken a world too bright to look on for long.

Her back to the work, she saw the magnesium light flash around the walls, heard the waspy sound, then turned to see the joining scar raised on the metal like a poker burn on skin. This was filed neatly, with a grating sound and sure strokes.

Then she examined the anvil, and a high workbench fitted with metal grips. Sometimes she was let turn the big screw and place a piece of timber under it. Jim showed her how to tighten it just the right amount but she wasn't very good. She preferred to play with the big pile of iron filings, heavy as blackened sand, teasing them, making them move as slowly as she could until all of a sudden they rushed to the big horseshoe shaped magnet, and clung, unable to resist. Magnetism. Jim explained it. She imagined a big field, oblong, with the magnets sticking up like lumps of rock, somewhere near the North Pole. It was called the magnetic field and it was so powerful it gave force to all the magnets in the world, in forges and batteries and cars, even the little play ones they got as toys.

The rock magnets were brown but the rest of the field was covered in moss. She knew it was ice, more likely, but it was hard to imagine a field of ice. She tried. The picture in her mind was too cold and it was a bad colour. Moss was better, with all the little filings rushing across the white expanse of the far north, like tiny rabbits, desperate to get home to their green velvety mother lode.

She'd wait around the forge forever in the hopes Jim would say 'Do you want to work the bellows?' The hearth was a few feet above floor level with an aperture for the air to come through. The bellows blew into that. She looked to him for approval, then stretching as high up as she could, onto her toes even, she grasped the wooden handle and pulled down with her full weight, her arms and chest straining. She'd hang there for one silent moment of struggle, then the great lung would begin to empty and sparks come from the bottom of the fire as she bore down. The handle would lift up and swing her with it, up and up until she see-sawed towards the ground again and the struggle was repeated. As her feet left the ground the fire puffed again. Soon there was rhythm. She'd set the fire blazing and her uncle added coal and later slack. When he said 'Good girl, that's enough' she stopped and wriggled her toes in her brown robin sandals, pleased, liking this more than any of the knitting or sewing she knew she'd never be able to master and never did.

Such was my ordinary life. But now let us look briefly at a different picture.

A yellow school bus moves away from the town of Clifden. The large rectangular back window is packed with the heads of adolescent boys. Their hair is carelessly cut; there is a suggestion of convicts or criminals. Two of them are making scary faces at the convent girls in their convent uniforms. Some of the girls are shivering in that exaggerated way schoolgirls have. The boys are 'the Frackers', wild, out of control. I was one of the girls. I shivered too but it was not the boys that scared me. It was the stories of a flock of wild boys, locked up in the care and control of the monks in the wilds of the mountains in Letterfrack. I had heard whispered stories of unmarked graves, of boys who ran away into the rain and the hills. This was in 1974.

Opening a College in such a place is an act of bravery and imagination. It is also, importantly, an act of reclamation. A deliberate turning from darkness to light.

This furniture is a work of triumph as well, on more than one level. Its decorative lightness is a delight, but I see it as a turning point, the products of minds and hands moving outwards, questing, unafraid.

Remember the horse in the forge? He came to mind when I visited the College and walked through the workshops where the basic skills are taught. I was shown the machines, sleek and steely and clean, and then the different types of wood, much of which is, not surprisingly, imported. Seán Treacy, who teaches students how to make the first contact between tools and material and introduces them to the basic skills, said something that got to the heart of it all. 'I want to teach them how timber moves,' he told me, and looking at the newly made tables and lamps, the basic furniture of our existence,

FURNISHING THE DETAILS (contd)

I was back in the forge, watching the line and beauty of a prancing, newly-shod white mare. Nowadays, there are the broader echoes of Dante and Homer, with their eloquent suffering trees, but the life in the material is what matters, the ability to work with or against the grain.

The College also teaches restoration. Here, a semi-restored piece of furniture reads like a cutaway map of the landscape, with slices of colour and material and social history laid bare. The materials used included horn, bone, and *pietra dura,* and I was not surprised that it takes one and a half years before a student works on an actual piece, as the safe manipulation of brittle material takes time, more so when such material is often expensive and rare. There was a fascinating amount of documentation and photography being done. One photograph of the bands of paint used on an old door was itself a work of abstract beauty and a perfect marriage of object and beauty.

The real achievement of the College is its marriage of craft and design. Students from one area can test their ideas and through consultation with skilled colleagues make necessary changes. Problems can be discussed from all angles. This is not only a desirable practical situation, but the basis of the most successful and sound teaching practice, that of group learning. This is where Letterfrack triumphs and the final pieces emerge beautifully crafted, as fine in execution as they are beautiful in conception. This is real work, in a place long starved of local industry, locally based training opportunities at third level. The student population is varied and drawn from many countries, which is not surprising in an area described by James Berry as being inhabited by ' … a race of mortals the most heterogeneous to be met with in Western Europe.'

'…So I chose to renew her, to rebuild, to prolong for a while the spliced yards of yesterday.'

So wrote Richard Murphy on the rebuilding of the last Galway hooker, an act which contributed in large measure to the repopulation of Summer bays with fleets of old sailing boats. The late Josie Connolly of Glinsk set up a training scheme for people learning to build boats and as a result, such schemes are now flourishing and young people learning the skill and art of the boatwright.

Who knows where an idea is forged, or how? Yet in this powerful landscape, informed by a vexed history, rich in the traditions and beauty of its own local crafts – and the boat is the supreme example of design and making to have graced and sustained Connemara North and South – past and future students will find sustenance.

Such a place has a way of entering the mind and the imagination. It's all to play for. Enjoy the show.

Mary O'Malley,
Seanbhaile,
Maigh Cuilinn.

July 2006.

Furnishing the Details

Course titles are coded as follows:

FCR B.Sc. in Furniture Conservation & Restoration
FDM B.Sc. in Furniture Design & Manufacture
FP B.Sc. in Furniture Production & Technology

All dimensions are in centimetres
The dimension sequence refers to Height x Length x Depth
All Conservation Projects © Private Collections
All Projects © GMIT at Letterfrack

↑ Peter Ranalow
Oak Bench
Oak and leather
60 x 148 x 36
21st Century Project
FDM2

The contrast of vertical and horizontal elements enhances the avant garde design of this bench. The blackened support, harmonised by the dark upholstered seats, acts as a form of decoration, and complements the rectilinear form by intersecting the horizontal element.

→ Alastair Creswell
Stand Alone Chair
Oak and red lacquer
116 x 44 x 37
Innovative Bathroom Furniture Project
FDM2

This slim line chair is design pared down to its bare minimum. Wall mounted or free standing, it can be used in any bathroom or apartment. The high-backed red frame acts like a spine, reflecting strong linear aesthetics and gives the structural elements an assured quality.

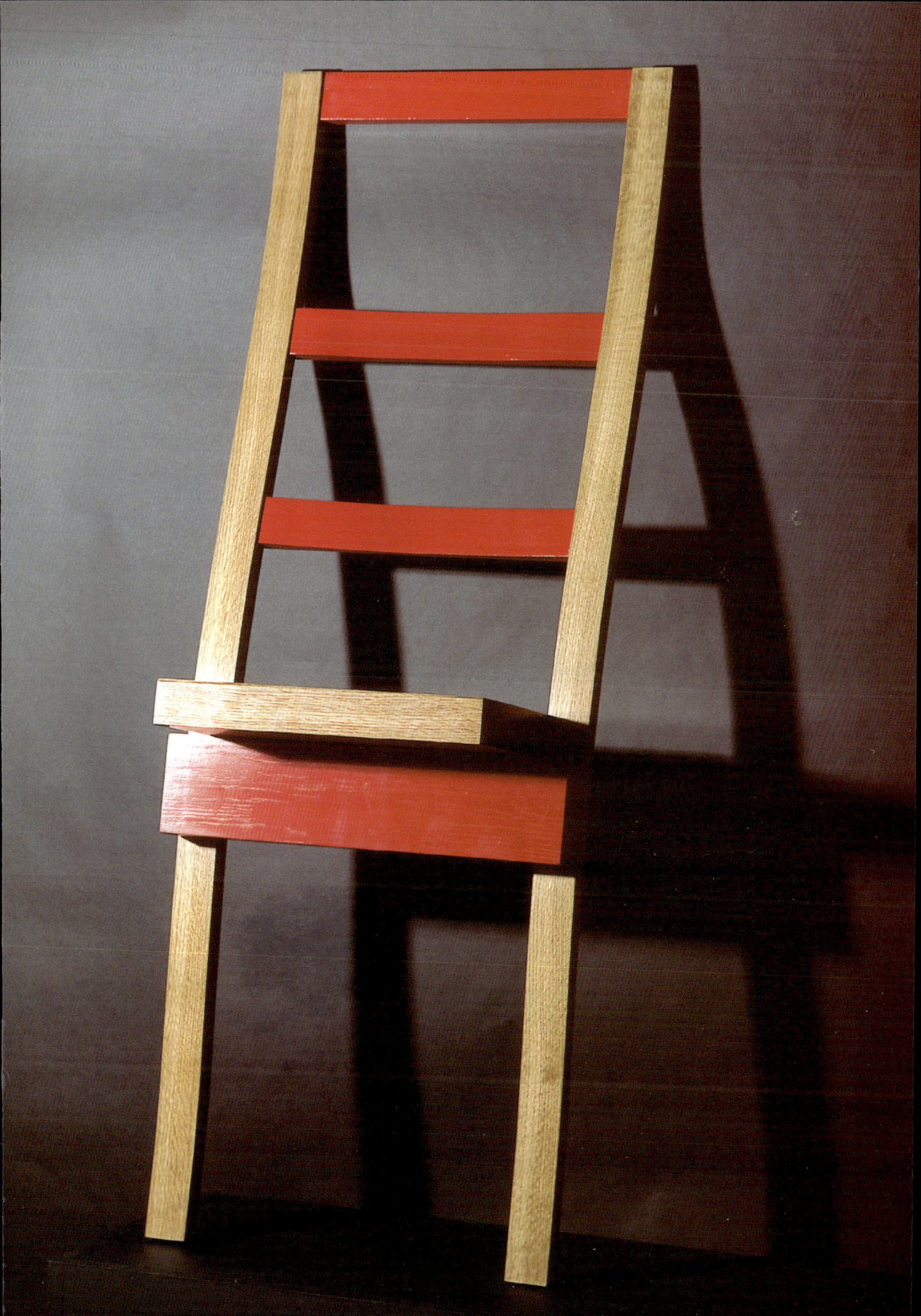

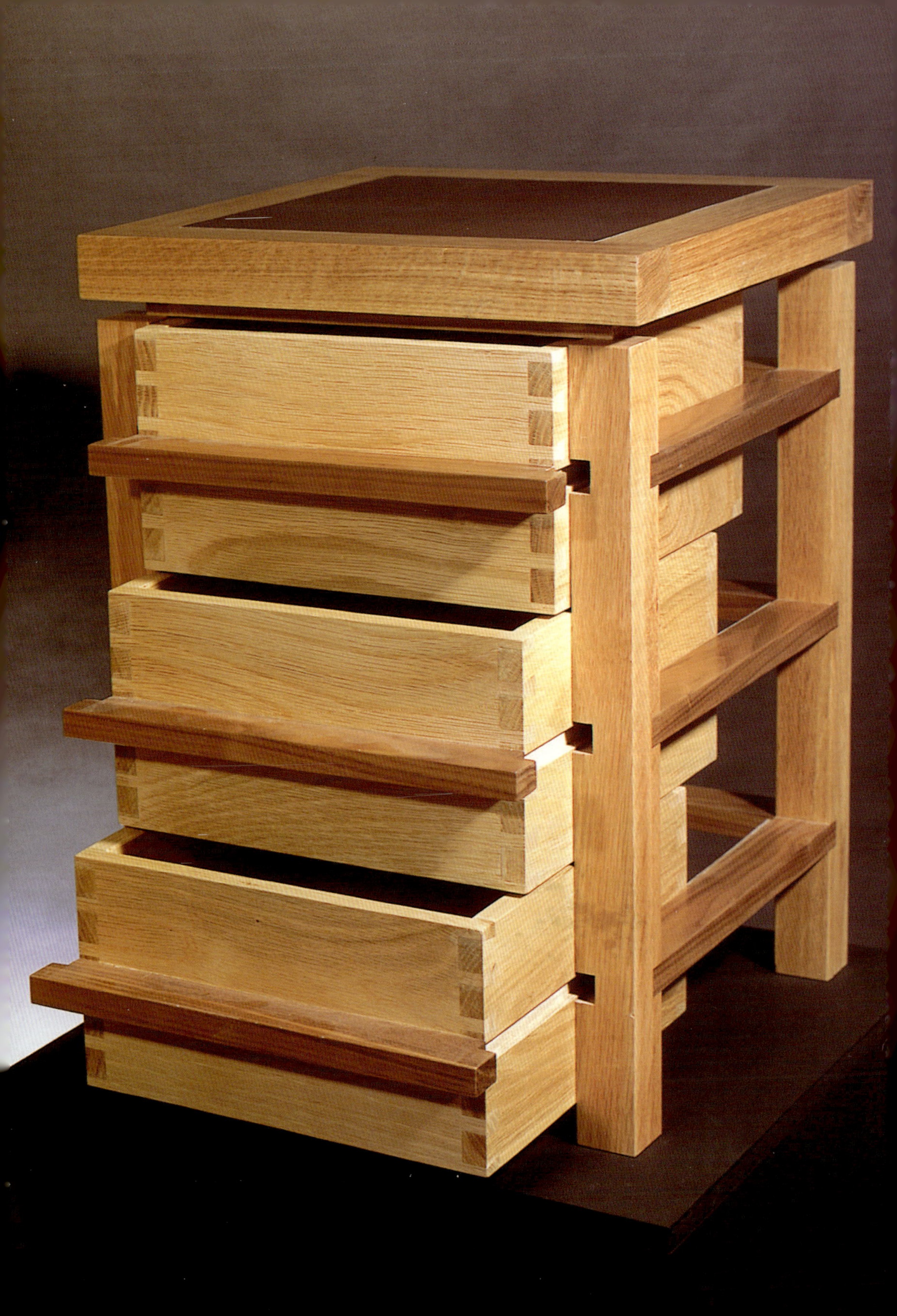

← Ryan Connolly
Bedside Storage Lockers
Oak, walnut and brown leather
63 x 44 x 44
Innovative Bathroom Project
FDM2

These bedside storage lockers are multi directional and are spatially adaptable to any particular interior. The use of different media adds to the illusion of depth, whilst the incorporation of the peak and trough effect on the front of the lockers displays a technical virtuosity and a sense of novelty.

↑ Martin Gallagher
Coffee Table with Integrated Stools
Plywood, steel, red leather and glass
46 x 72 x 72
21st Century Project
FDM2

The use of modern materials imparts a contemporary character to this coffee table ensemble. The multifunctional seats contain a storage system, their cylindrical forms complement the curved lines of the plywood table, while transparent glass and vivid upholstery provide a visual balance and harmony.

↑ Henning Schulze
Souvenir Box in the Mudejar Style
Bone (red stained), pewter, rosewood, ebony, green stained poplar, maple, walnut, brass and olive wood
8 x 31 x 11
Conservation Project
Staff
Decorated in the Mudejar style, this 20th century box comes from the Iberian Peninsula or North Africa. Through removing a dark varnish and finishing with a layer of wax the planar surfaces of the wood are enlivened. This emphasises the complementary techniques used to create the complicated geometric patterns.

→ Peter Drumm
End Grained Chair
Oak
90 x 42 x 50
21st Century Project
FDM2
The atypical, patterned grain of this chair creates an ingenious trompe l'oeil effect. The clean lines add a sense of refinement and convincingly draw the eye to the cantilevered seat and inclining back. Strength, tension and sturdiness are achieved by hidden support bars to the rear.

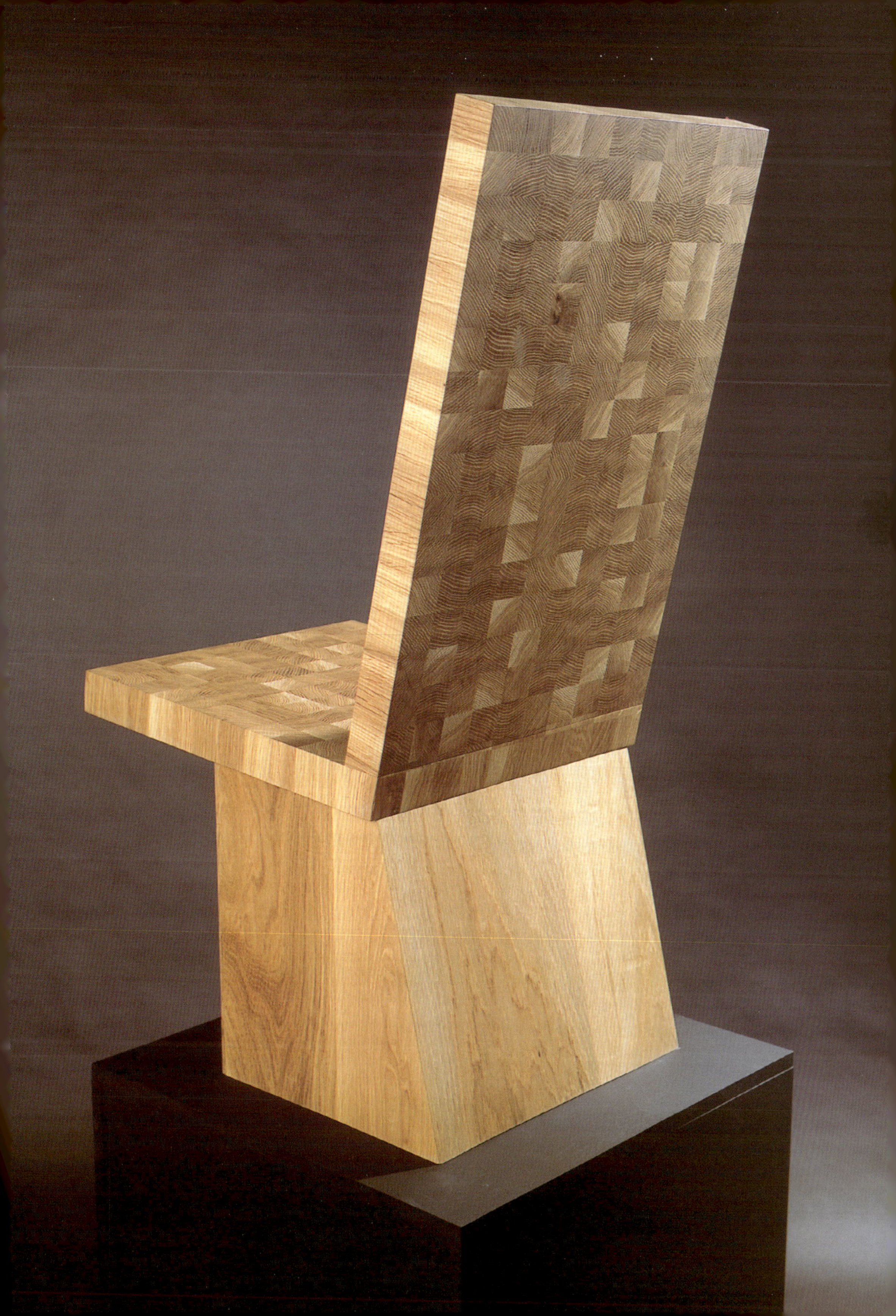

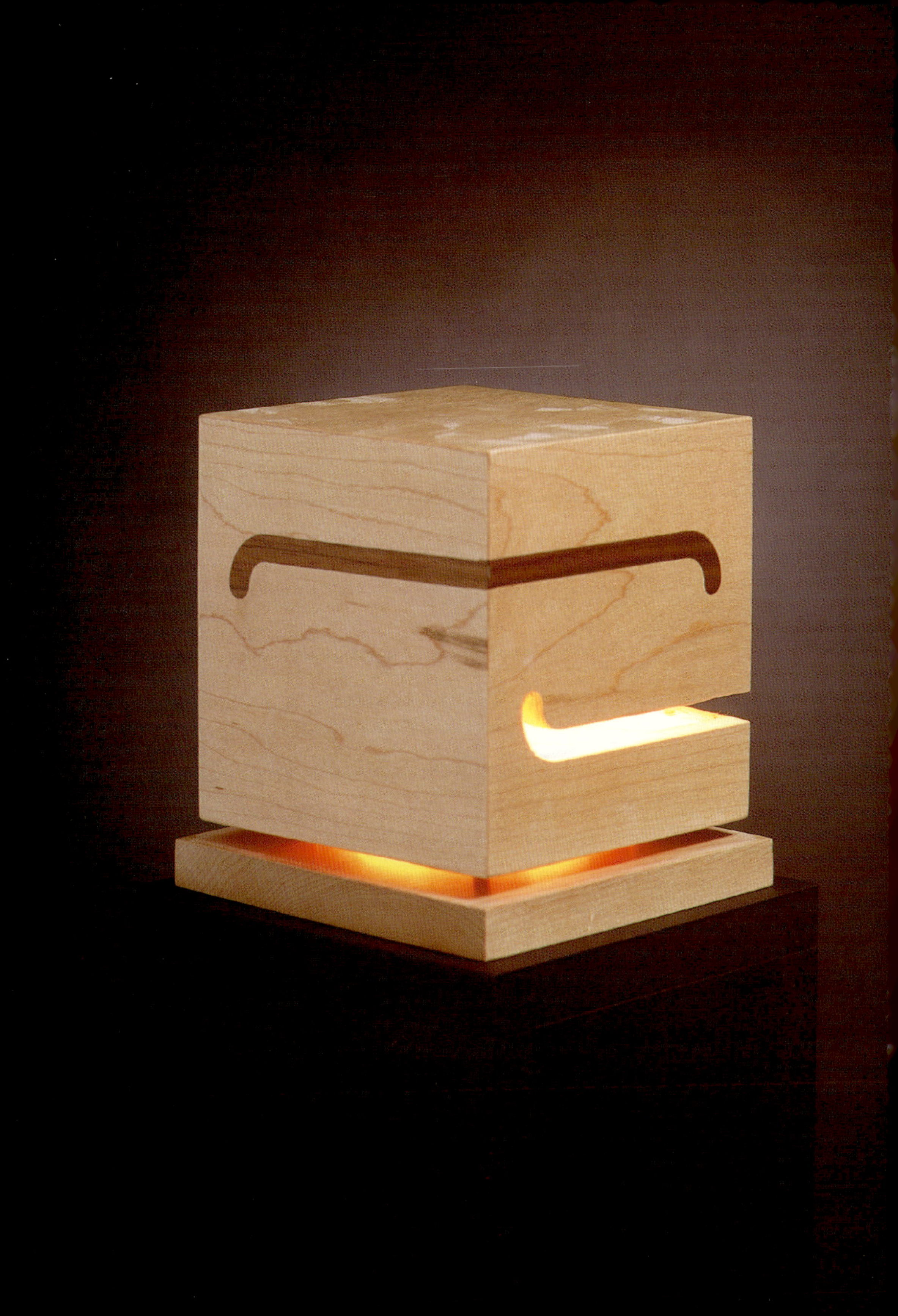

← Seán Cusack and Thomas J. Donnellan
Cube Light
Maple and walnut
14 x 13 x 13
Corporate Gift Project
FP2 and FDM2

This design is an exercise in simplicity, elegance and utility. A batch of twenty was produced combining CNC and electrics into the design. The translucent streamlined sections turn this cube into a luminescent object, mysterious and practical at the same time.

↑ Morgan Lalor
CD Holder
Walnut, walnut veneer and birch plywood
52ø x 15
Lamination Project
FP2

This versatile holder is quite different from standard unit furniture as it eschews the repeats of geometric patterns. Instead, the concept is derived from the music industry, as the various shelves and compartments represent the different types of music which exist.

FURNISHING THE DETAILS

↑ Declan Brangan and Peter Ranalow
Mood Light Box
Oak and white lacquered MDF
13.5 x 10 x 10
Corporate Gift Project
FP2 and FDM2
This simple cubic form exploits the design potential of this product to the full. The brief for the design of this ambient desk light was to create a high quality corporate gift. The vertical recesses in the body of the lamp complement the horizontal beam of light.

→ Kate Dunne and Ryan Connolly
Cube Light Box
Birch plywood
13 x 12 x 12
Batch Production Project
FP2 and FDM2
This lamp is exceptional through the subtle integration of four cut out horizontal lines, each slightly wider than the last, which reveal the internal light source. Soft lighting contrasts with sharp edges. Its dimensions and perfect proportioning were determined by the Fibonacci sequence.

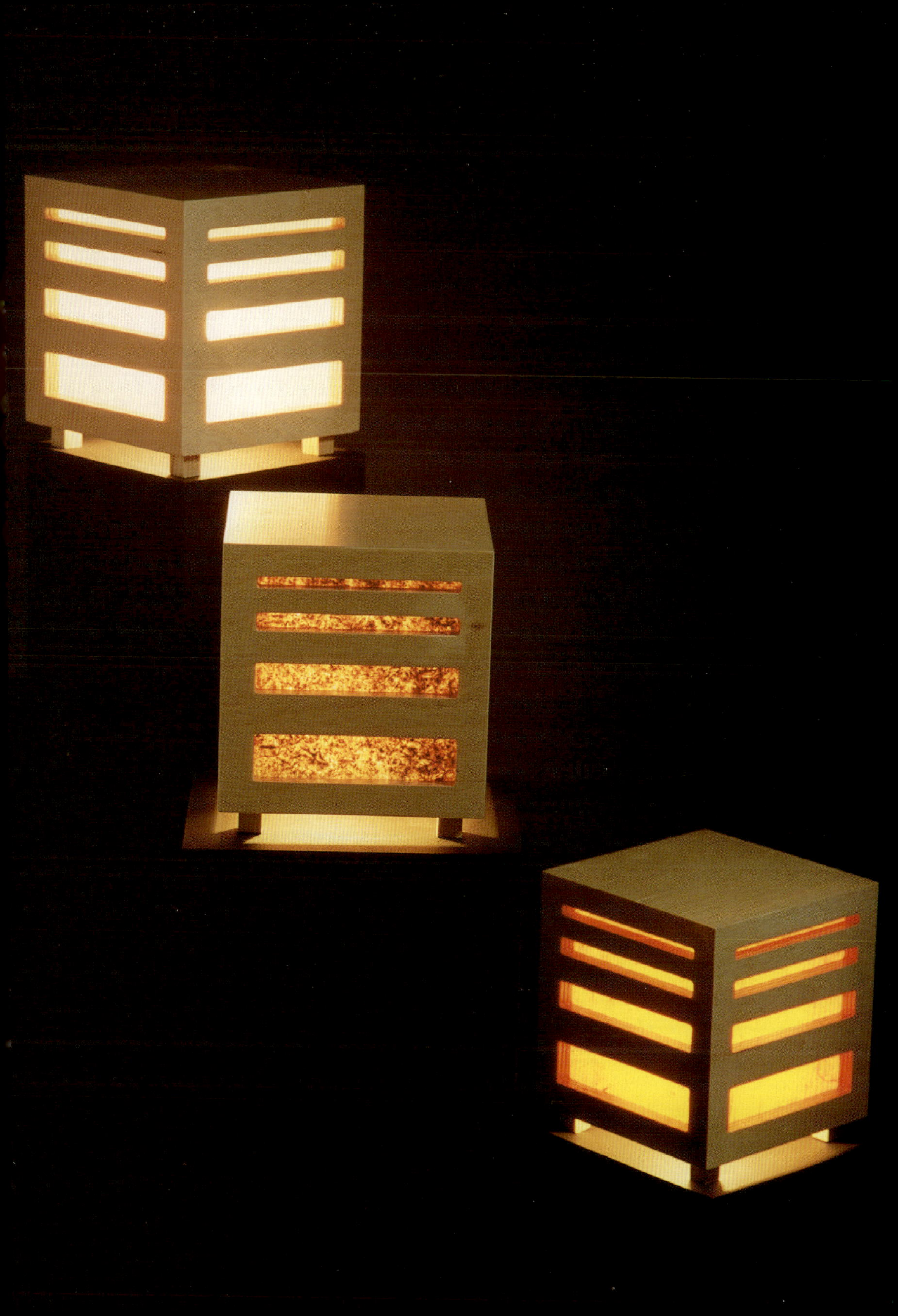

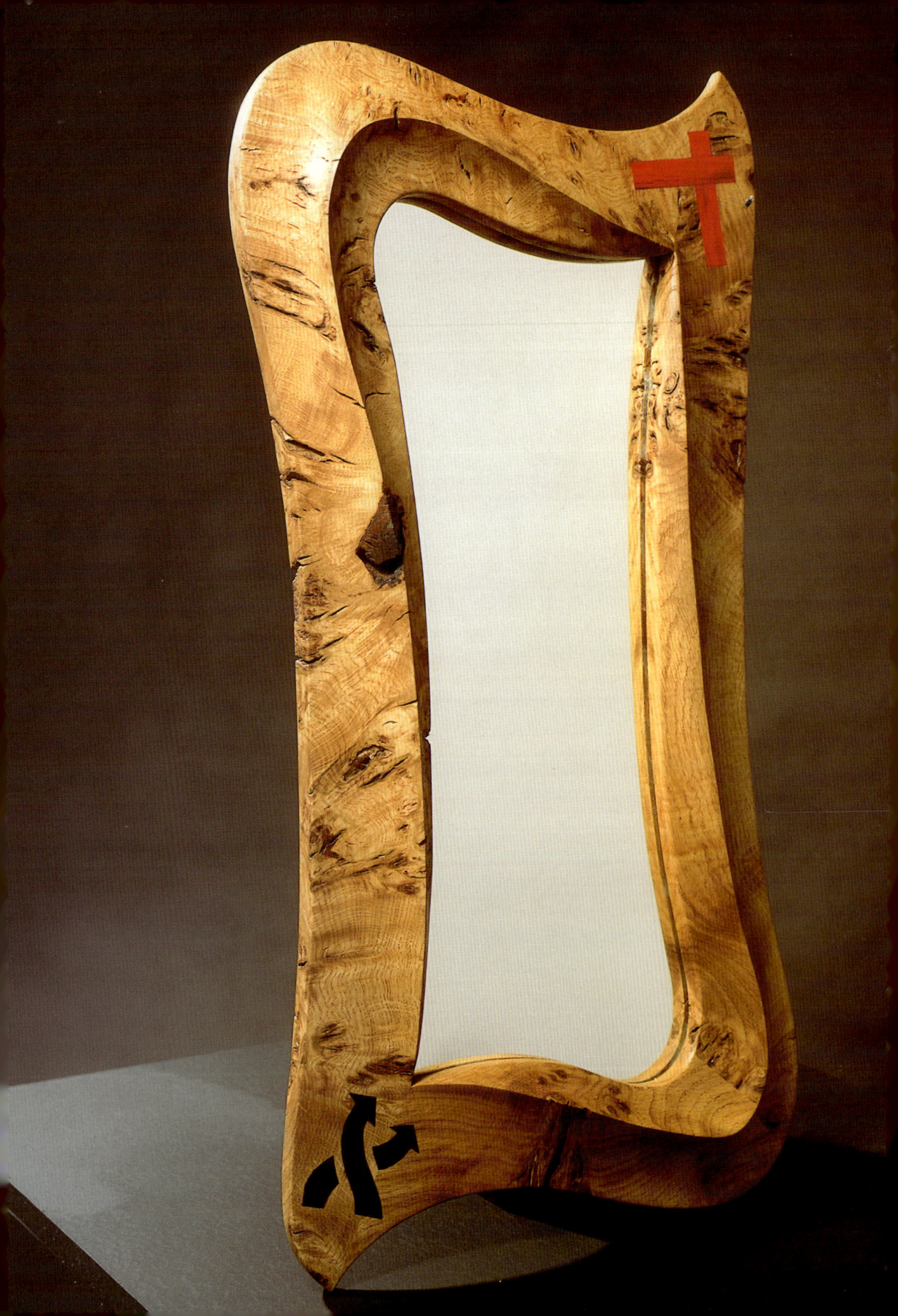

← Ian McDermott
Mirror – A reflection of the Inner Person
Oak
63 x 33.5 x 4
Design and Make - Final Project
FDM1

The various media and symbols reflect the client's personality. The undefined height of the mirror represents the tumultuous journey in the choice of a career. Inlaid with bog oak, the arrows epitomise ambiguity and indecision. The red cross signifies the client's final chosen profession – nursing.

↑ Alan Treacy
Turned Lamps
Walnut, maple, cherry, oak and ash
Varying heights 23 – 33 cm with 9 cm ø
Commission Project
Graduate

The project brief stipulated utilising solid, quality Irish materials in the design and manufacture of a product. The design expresses creativity, simplicity and originality. The neutral coloured lamp shades uses suede or Irish linen. Combined with complementary dark and light woods, its cylindrical form provides choice and variety for any interior.

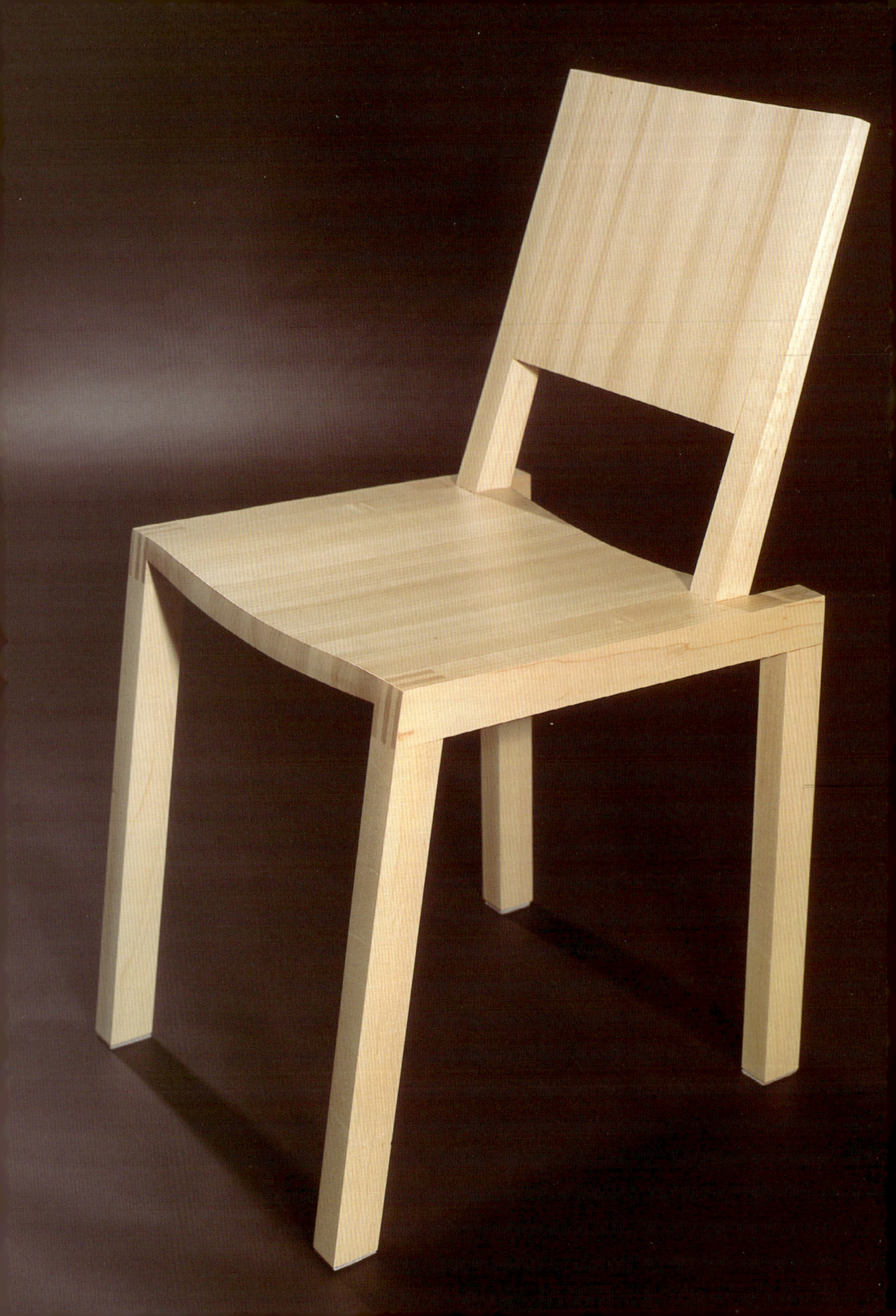

← Brian Cooney
Chair
Maple
78 x 40 x 40
21st Century Project
FDM2

This neat kitchen chair is made from solid maple. All components join flush, enhancing its modern architectural appearance. The seat and back support, made in a similar way to traditional wooden barrels, used narrow lengths of maple with a 1° angle off square, producing a suitable gentle curve.

↑ Ryan Connolly
Marquetry Panel
Elm, burr maple and lacewood
13 x 13
Marquetry Project - Theme: Time
FDM2

The simplicity of the decorative scheme on this panel is unquestionable. The spiralling geometric, stylised pattern is inspired by infinity and is brought to life through the clever combination of the various woods. Its production reflects the designer's virtuosity expressed in the entirety of the panel.

↑ Martin Gallagher
Marquetry Panel
Maple and walnut veneer and Macassar ebony
27 x 19.5
Marquetry Project - Theme: Time
FDM2

Representing a passage through time, the ebony symbolises the vague early years of the designer's life, whilst the use of walnut and maple signify the clarity of later years. The inspiration for this panel came from Op artists Victor Varsley and Bridget Reilly.

↗ Brendan McAuliffe
Marquetry Panel
Lacewood and black dyed veneer
20.5 x 29
Marquetry Project - Theme: Time
FDM2

This panel shows an appreciation of materials. The figuring of the wood is essential to its success as it forms the essence of its decorative effect. Technically the marquetry appears vibrant through the contrasts of the wood and veneer, illustrating the integrity of its construction.

→ Brian Cooney
Marquetry Panel
Walnut and maple
21 x 31
Marquetry Project - Theme: Time
FDM2

This panel is an abstract interpretation of time. Appearing like a perspective drawing each channelled area could represent people, planets or universes. The patterns create a textured effect and the diaphanous quality of the marquetry results in a most distinctive piece.

26 | FURNISHING THE DETAILS

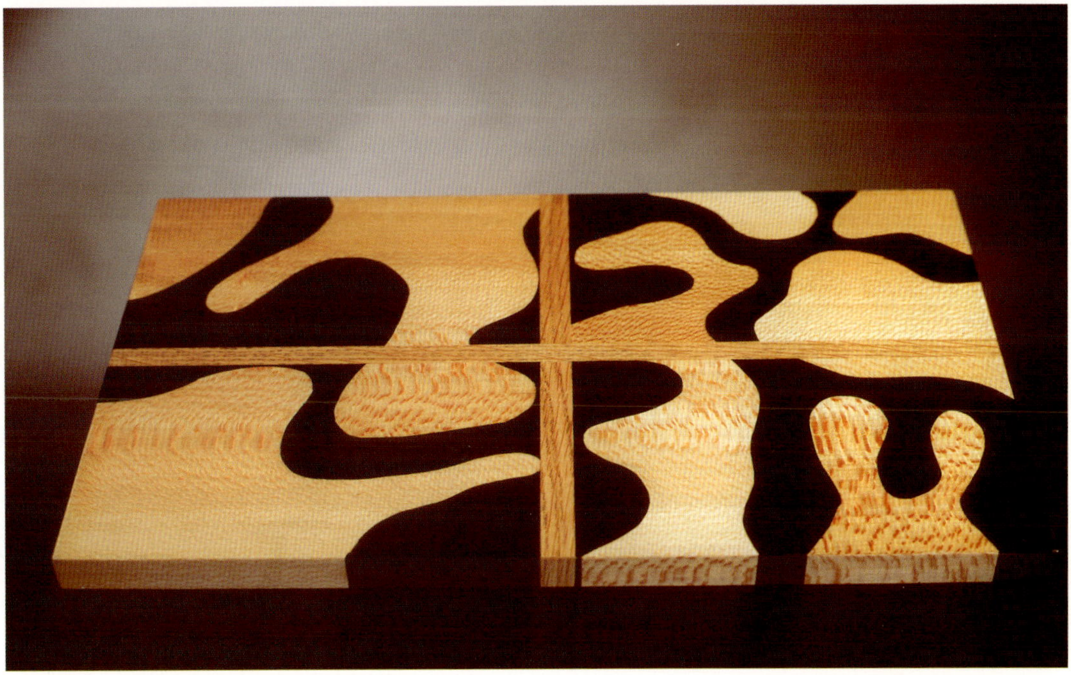

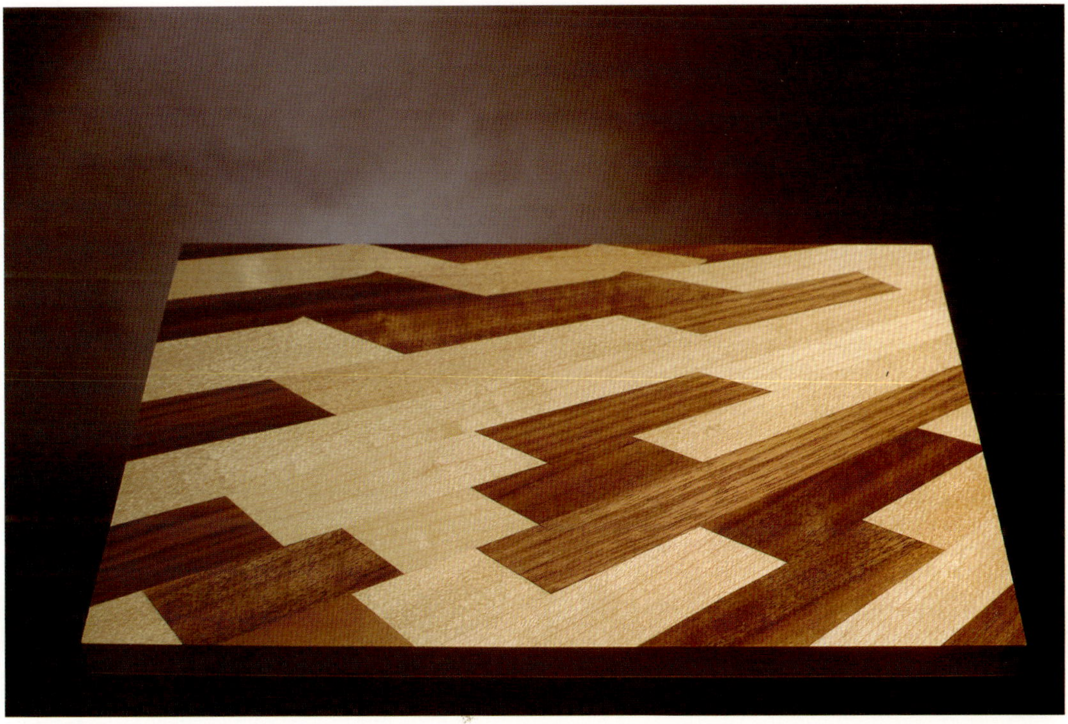

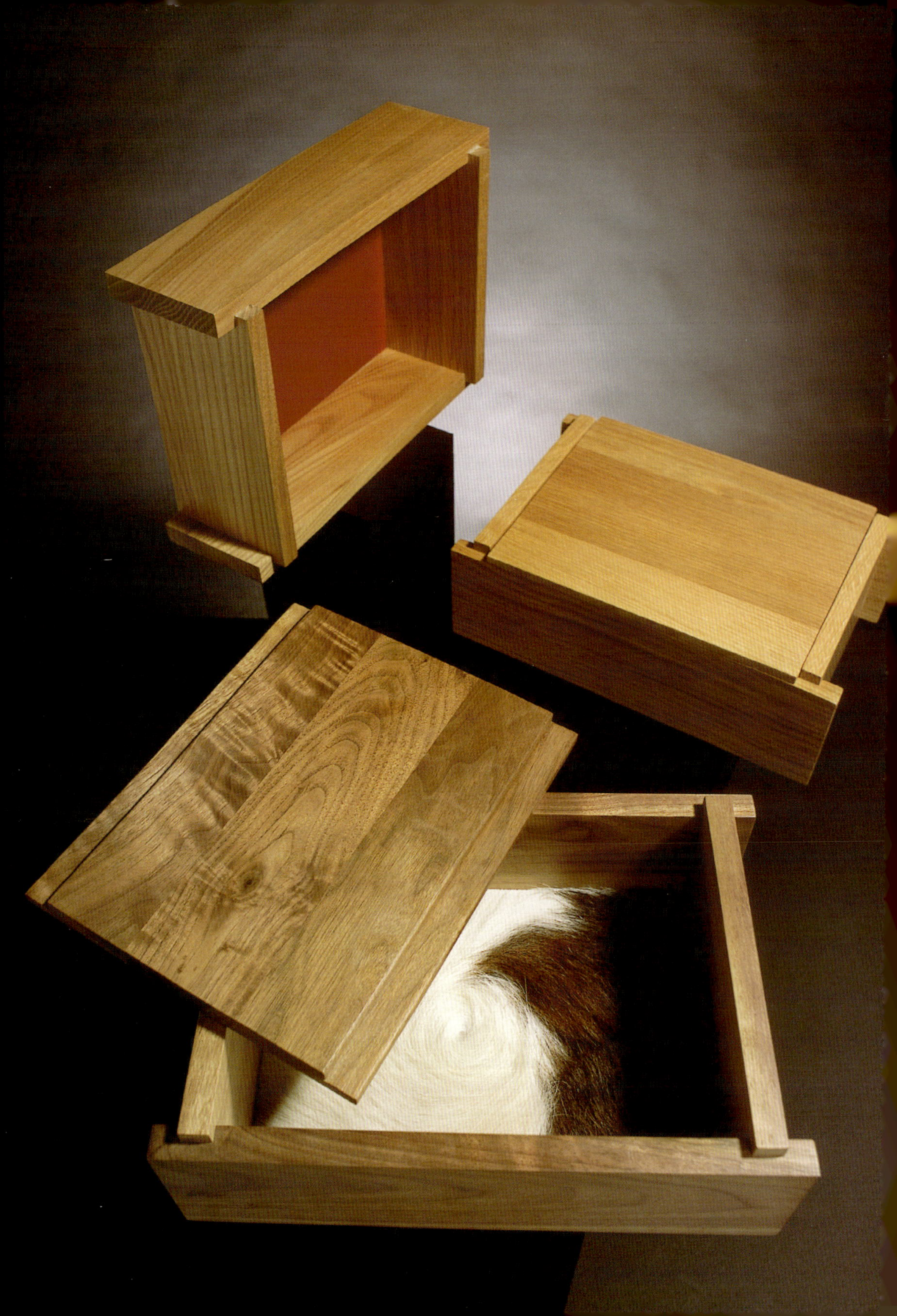

← Liam Connor and Patrick Carty
Trinket Boxes
Elm, oak, walnut, lined with leather, suede or cow hide
10 x 30 x 20
Skills Development Project
FP1
Each student adhered to a classic design for this trinket box. The materials chosen complied with the project brief. Each chose to use a unique wood with a different lining, creating a simple unadorned wood exterior which contrasts with the sensuous material and colour of the interior.

↑ Sarah O'Sullivan, Maurice Molloy and Gillian Goodbody
Cutlery Canteens (before and after treatment)
Mahogany veneer, sycamore, tulipwood, pine, brass (silver plated), steel, bone and baize
34 x 22 x 28
Conservation Project
Graduate
With a typical serpentine shape and sloping lid these deep Georgian canteens are composed of pine with a mahogany veneer and an oak base, with baize glued to the underside. Consolidation of a misaligned lower substructure, replacement of missing chequered banding and veneers, and removal of a dark, unoriginal varnish, reinstated their original condition.

↑ Simon Brown and Oliver Prigoda
Sofa Table
Mahogany, ebony, brass and fire gilding
68 x 149 x 66
Conservation Project
Graduate and FCR2

The objective of this project was the treatment of the unstable substructure, detached veneers and the finish. Various parts were loose. The central focus was the preservation of the original French polish. Separating original shellac layers were re-adhered to the substrate and areas of loss were filled before minimal re-polishing.

→ Rory Tangney
Dragonfly
Walnut and cherry
126 x 137 x 34
Gallery Piece
Graduate

This stylised dragonfly displays a sensual wisdom of form. The sheer size of the piece suggests an organic rhythm in that it might actually take flight. This work successfully demonstrates the biodynamic qualities of the materials and the structural qualities of the piece.

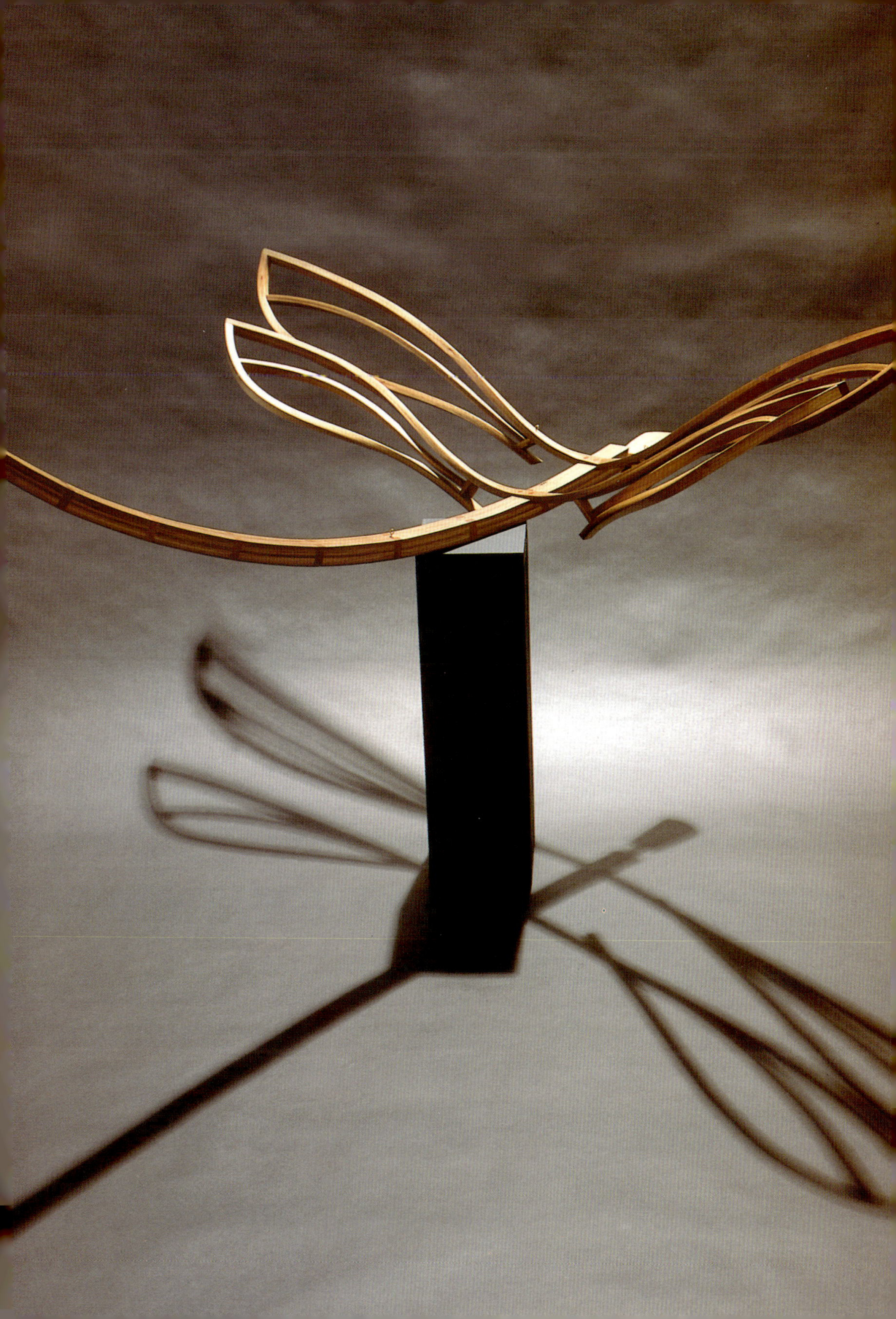

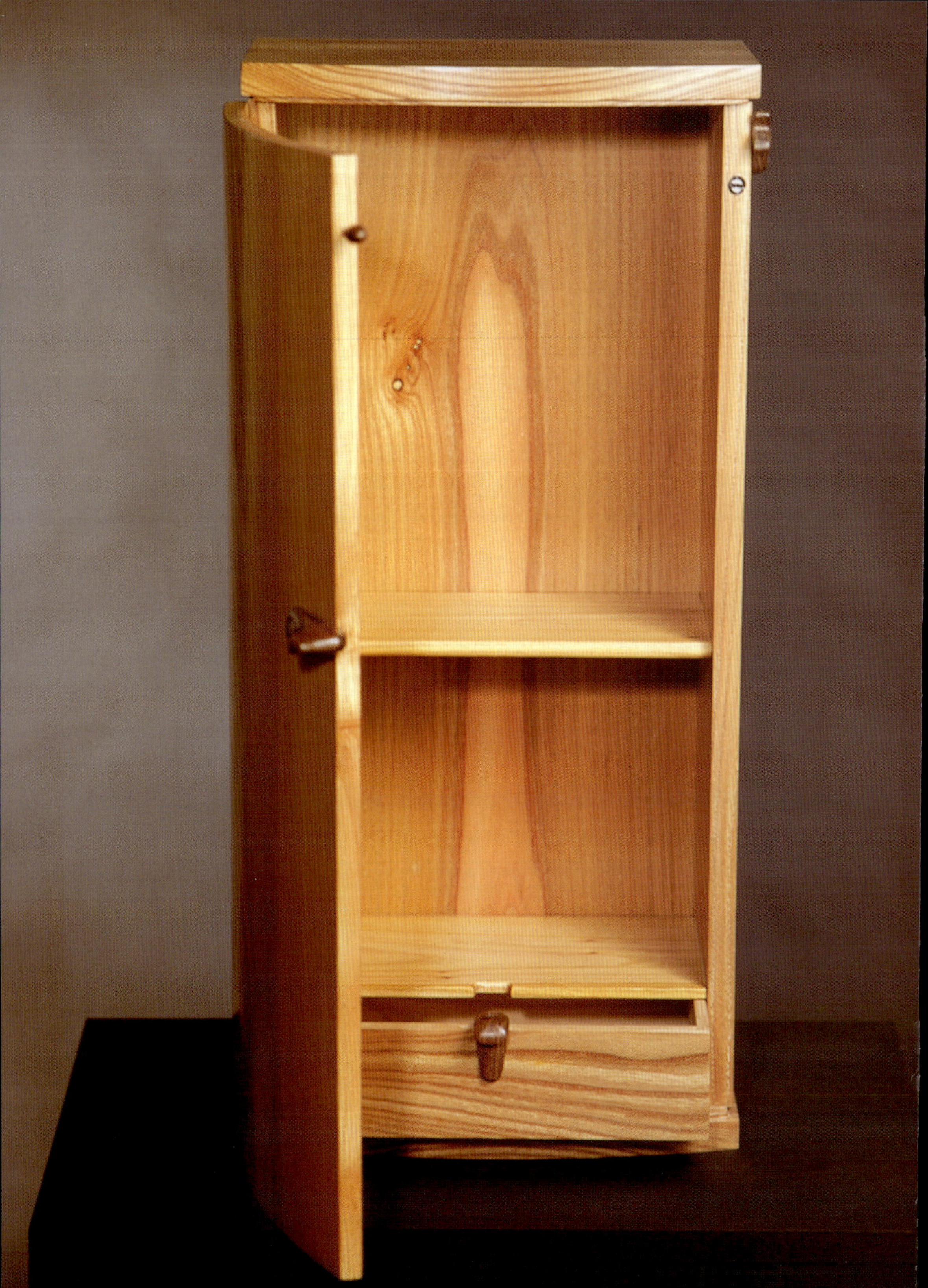

←P. J. Murphy
Curved Wall Cupboard
Elm
59 x 17.5 x 29
Cabinet Project, Furniture Making Project I
FDM1

The design for this curved wall cupboard is cunningly masterful. The celebration of the wood, the sleek emphasis of the grain and the use of wooden handles highlight its unique sensibility. It was designed specifically to store small, precious items.

↑ James Lonergan
Sofa Table
Oak and lacquered MDF
51 x 52 x 38
21st Century Project
FDM2

This user friendly table was suitably designed for a modernist interior. Comfortable to use, through its incisive lines and strong exploitation of colour, it is visually agreeable. The laminated oak rails create a stable frame, and the curvature of the legs provides visual awareness by creating a shadow.

FURNISHING THE DETAILS | 33

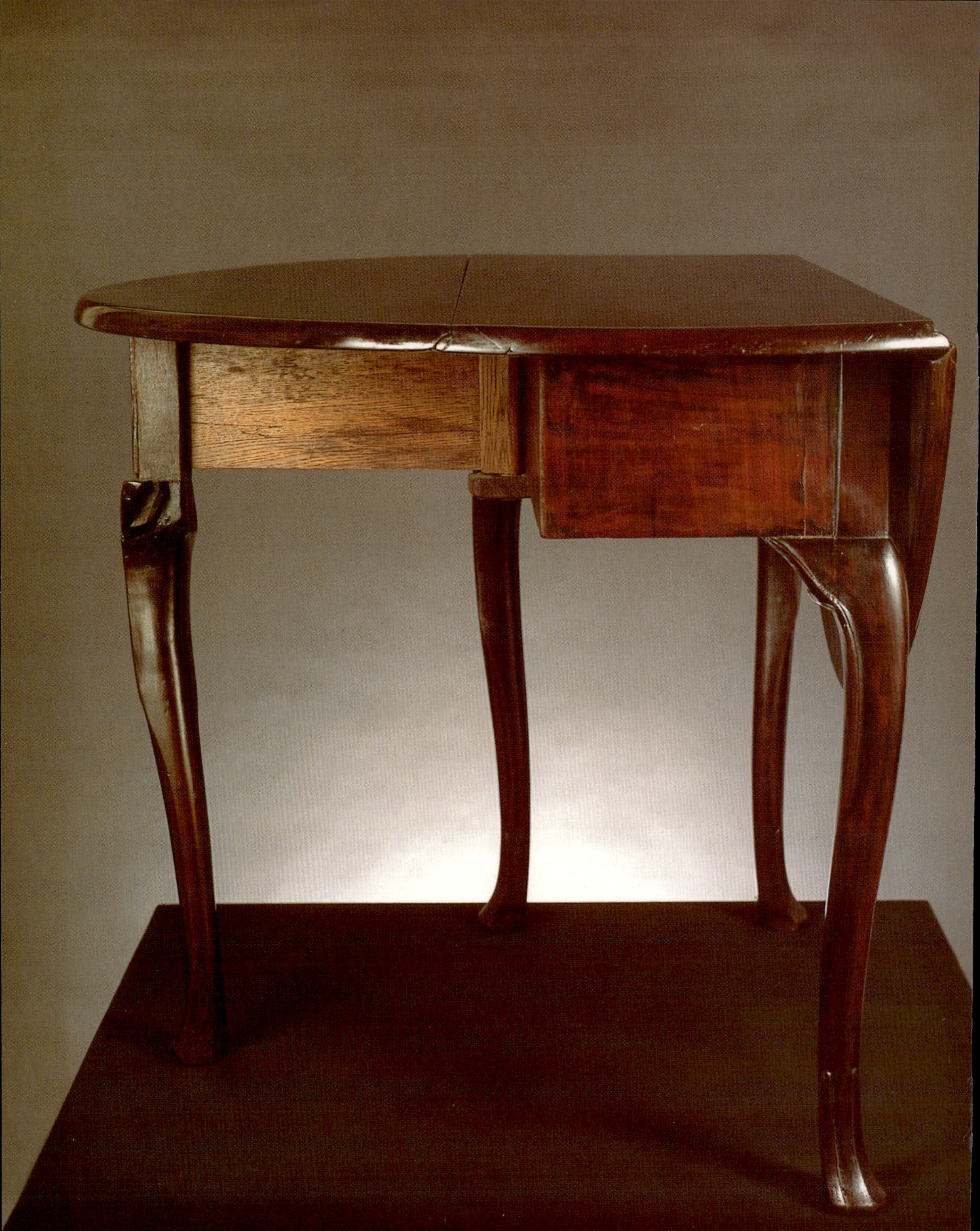

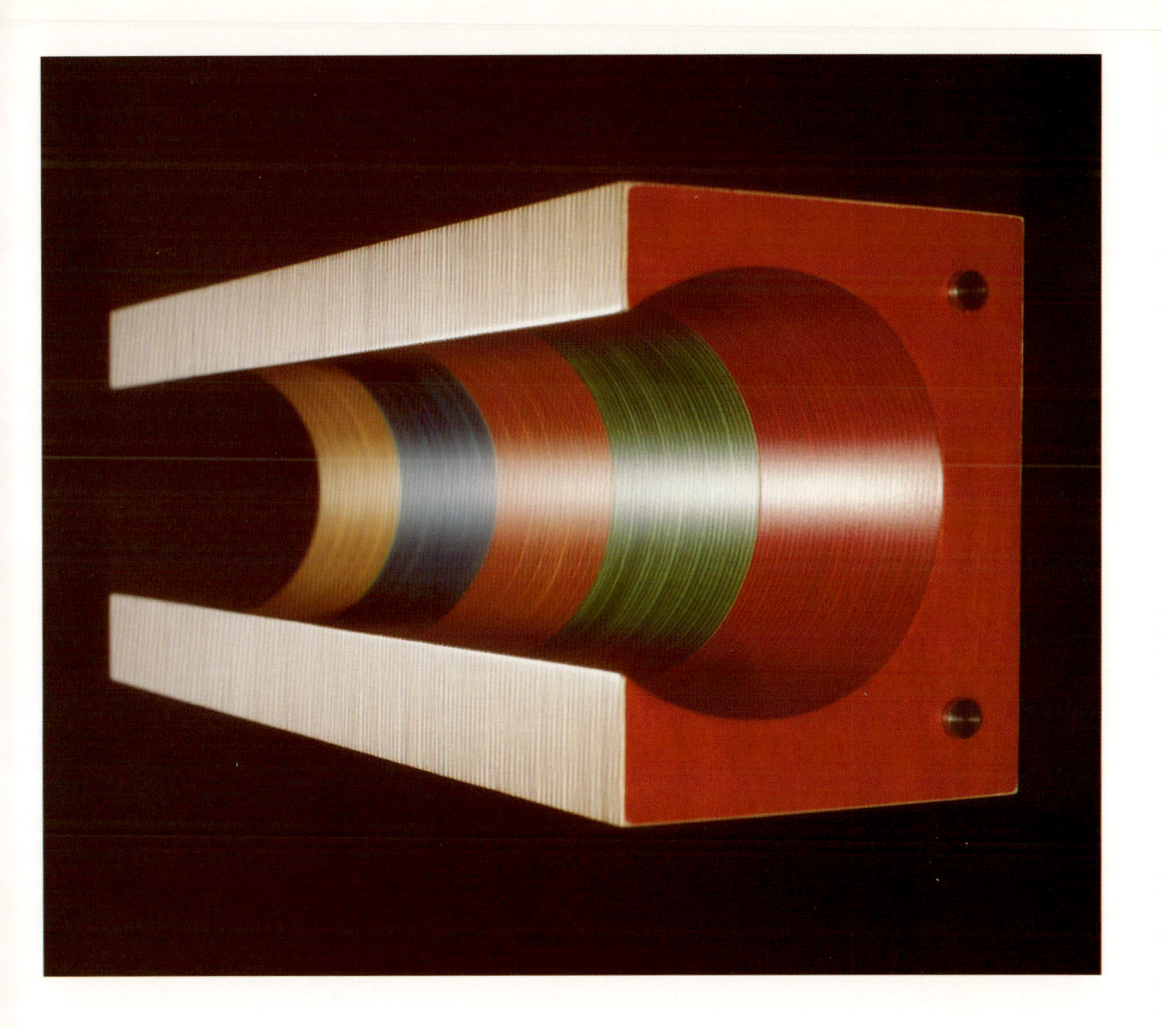

← Mercie Hogan
Irish Drop Leaf Table
Mahogany and oak
72 x 106 x 94
Conservation Project
Graduate

Dating approximately 1750 this oval table was dismantled and reassembled, with missing areas refilled in mahogany. An idiosyncratic leg joining was recarved. The 'fly leg' swivel mechanism was repaired. The typical dark varnish was in-painted and hand varnished. The later-added, uneven finish of the top was thinned and polished.

↑ Martin Gallagher
Striped Shelf
Birch plywood, fabric dyes and stainless steel
14 x 44 x 11
Innovative Bathroom Project
FDM2

This striped shelf articulates simplicity, yet achieves maximum impact, primarily through minimalism. The distinctive cut and fold of the curve is inspired by the motion of the sea. The sycophantic sincerity of the design is realised by the combination of colour and wood.

↑→ Brigid Sealy
Chair Bench
Beech
86 x 46.5 x 54
Innovation Project
Graduate

This stylish chair extends easily into a bench for two people. Inspired by innovative folding garden furniture it is made from solid beech with brass fittings. The soft, delicate grain of the wood is highlighted by the use of a glossy, satin lacquer finish.

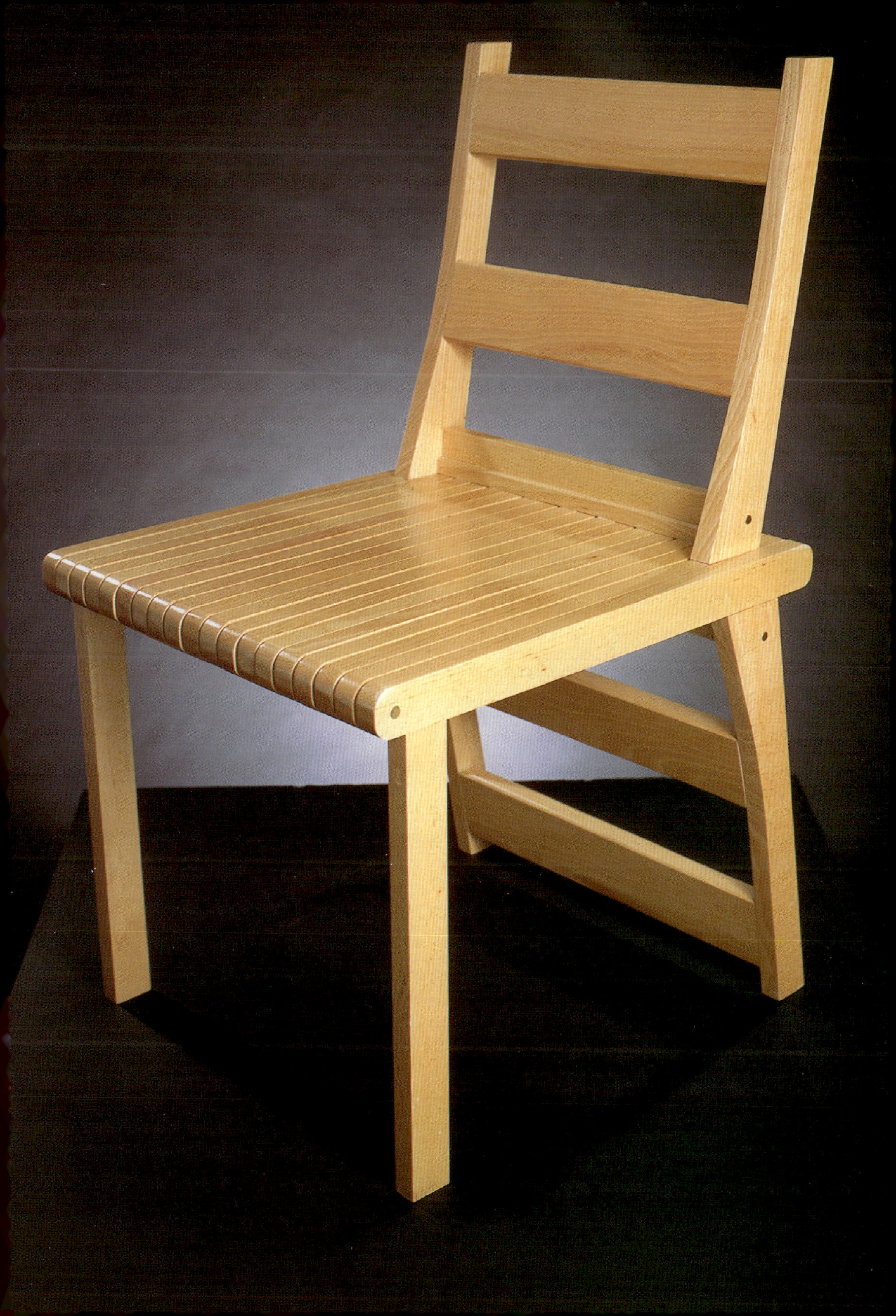

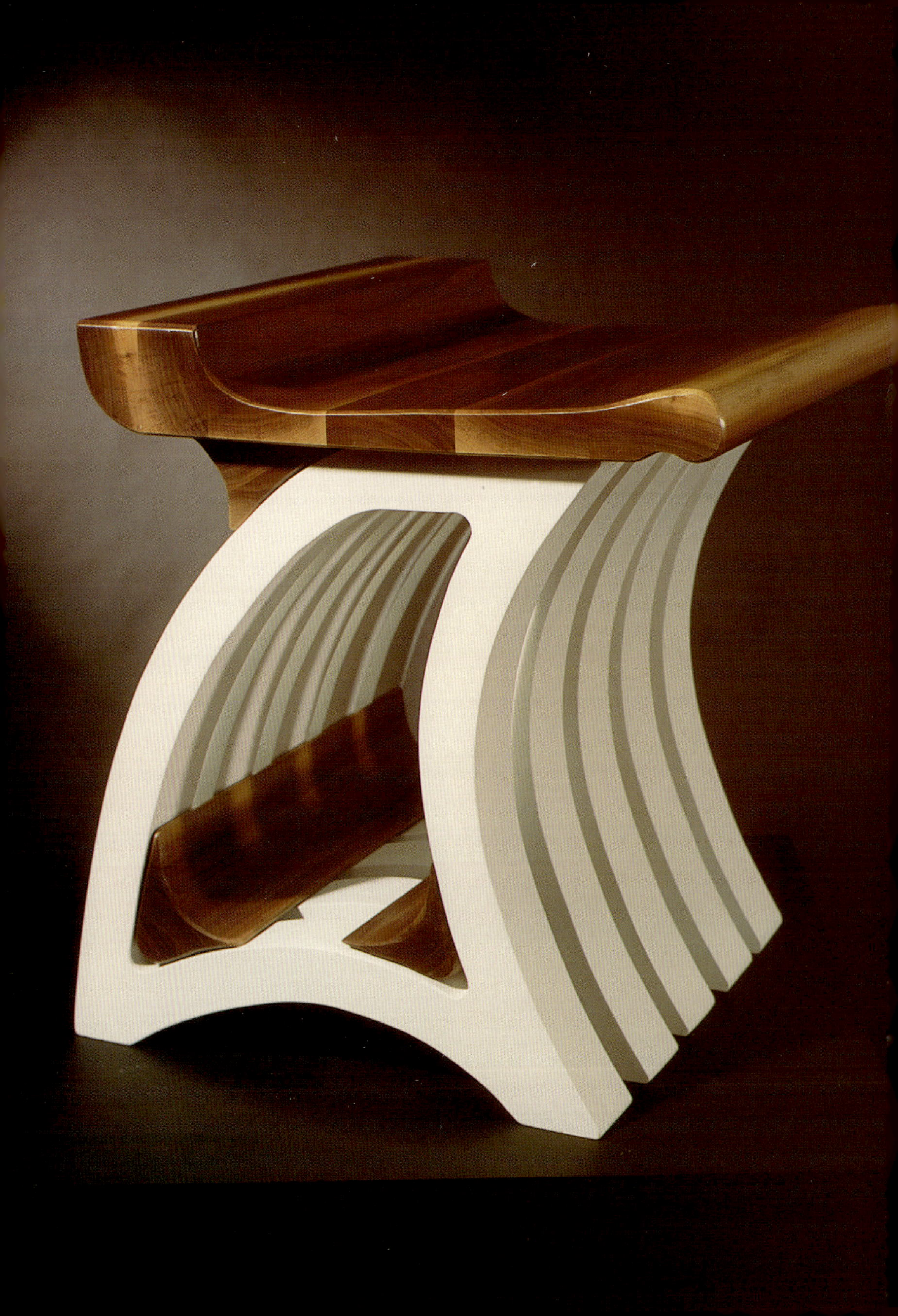

← Shane Tubrid
Walnut Stool
Walnut and white lacquered MDF
46 x 40 x 40
Innovative Bathroom Furniture Project
FDM2
The unique sensibility of this walnut stool with white base reflects the modernist penchant for undulating forms and light, bright colours. The seat, specifically shaped for comfort, and the idiosyncratic curves of the base align with the totality of the design.

↑ Rory Tangney
Wood Sculpture - Awakening
Beech
90.5 x 43 x 33
Gallery Piece
Graduate
This sculpture is representative of the hope and joy experienced through nurturing and realising dreams and potentials. Reflecting constructivist tendencies, it casually dissolves linear forms into a swirling mass, grounding the piece of sculpture with its mass, weight and centre.

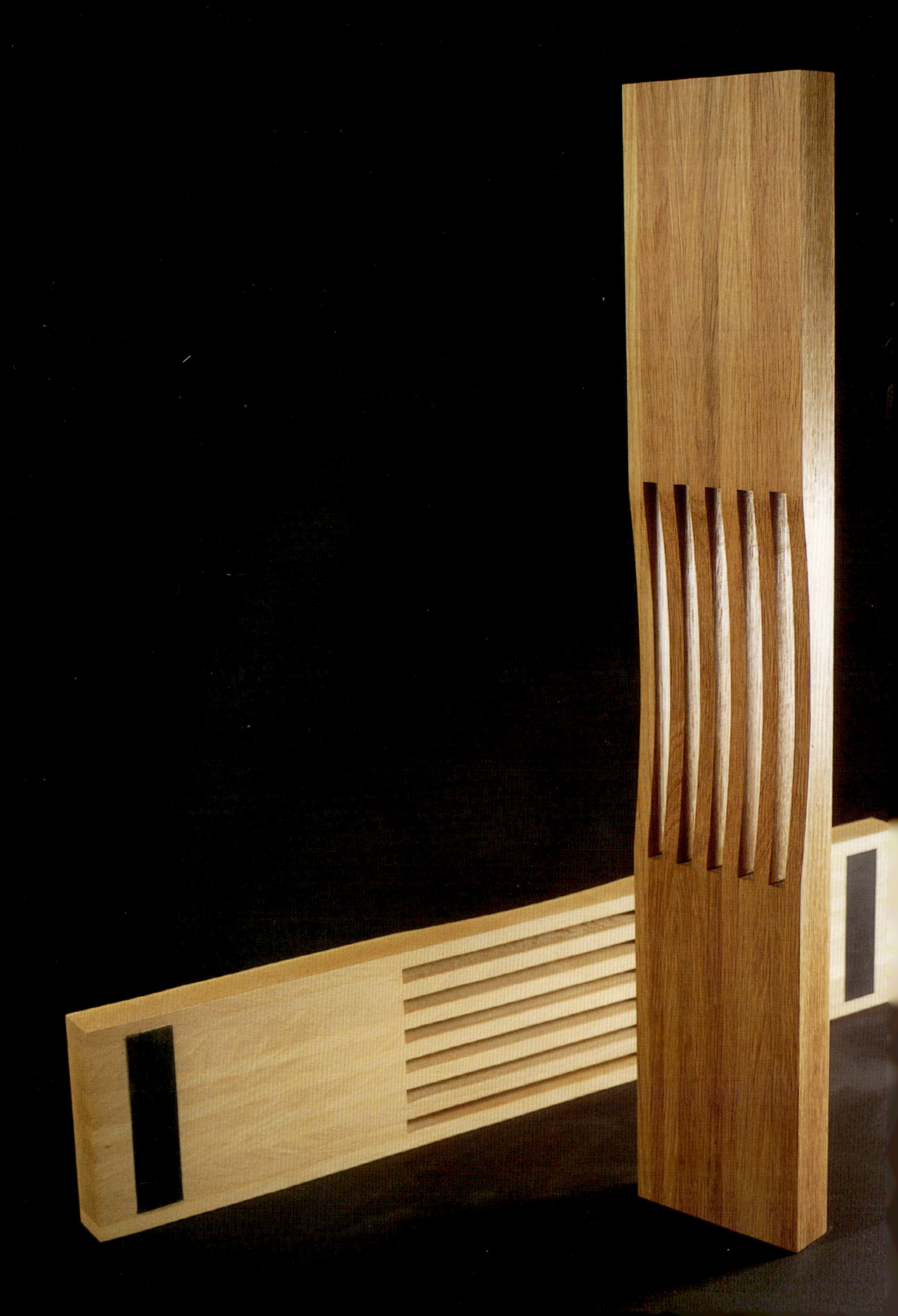

← Brian Cooney
Bath Tray
Oak and beech
4 x 76 x 14
Innovative Bathroom Furniture Project
FDM2
This simple bathroom accessory creates a shelf for bathing products and middle grate for wet items. It is constructed from thirty one narrow lengths of wood in oak and beech. It is finished in a water resistant tung nut oil which enhances the functionalism of the piece.

↑ Ryan Connolly
Storage Cabinets
Walnut, cherry, constructional veneer and MDF
43 x 73 x 8
Innovative Bathroom Furniture Project
FDM2
These storage cabinets with linking inlays are inspired by the golden rectangle. Based on the dimensions of the golden ratio, which claimed to be the most aesthetically pleasing shape of a rectangle, the simplicity of the lines and the contrasting woods reinforce their mathematical precision.

↑ Seán Burns
Le Boume Coffee Table
Beech, glass and metallic paint
46.5 x 117 x 66
21st Century Project
FDM2

The bold cartoon-like sculptural design and expressive colours are characterised through three sinuous biomorphic forms. Each is carved from steamed beech, finished in automotive paint and lacquer with a nine millimetre glass top. The impact of this form psychologically evokes sentiments of harmony and self-esteem.

→ John Ryan
Vertical Shower
Softwood, steel tubing, metallic paint and fountain pump
230
Innovative Bathroom Furniture Project
FDM2

Organic in form, this shower is both visually and functionally innovative. Its ergonomic design contains a fountain pump which projects the water upward. Upon contact with each shower head the water is dispersed. There are three different heights of shower head. Each is accessible by turning the tube.

FURNISHING THE DETAILS

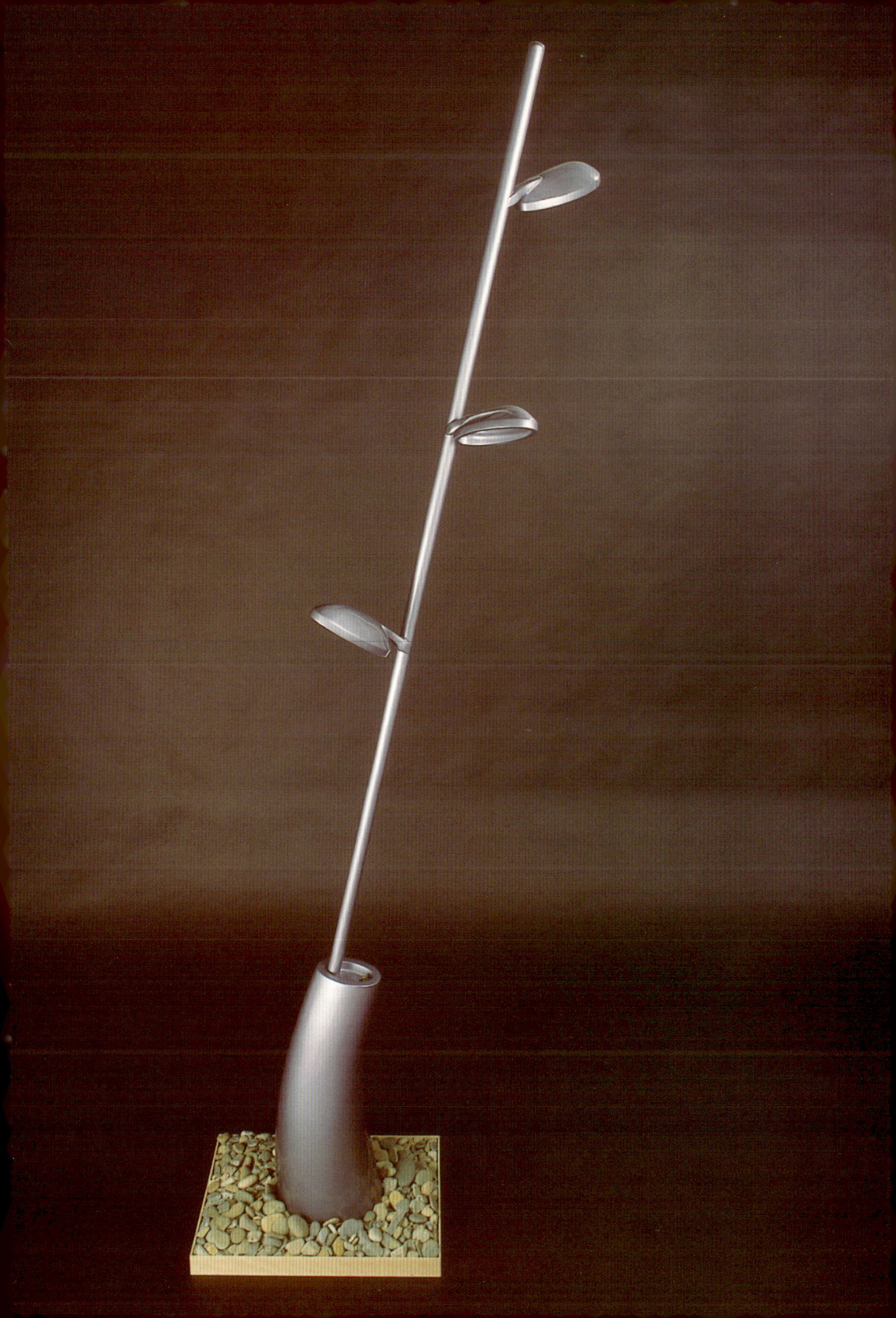

↑ Noel Whelan
Jewellery Boxes
Burr walnut and birch ply
4 x 21.5
CNC Project
FP2

These boxes reflect an appreciation of materials and form. The marbled wood is integral to the success of the boxes as an ensemble, forming the basis of their decorative effect. When the six compartments are amalgamated their circular form does not compromise the lustre of the wood.

→ Noel Whelan
CD Rack
Walnut and oak
33 x 38 x 19
Lamination Project
FP2

The primordial form is a characteristically simple idea. Its fluid lines produce an aesthetic yet functional curve used to hold the compact discs. A tension is maintained in the continuous flow of the wood. This dynamic design results in a streamlining effect and an anomalous style.

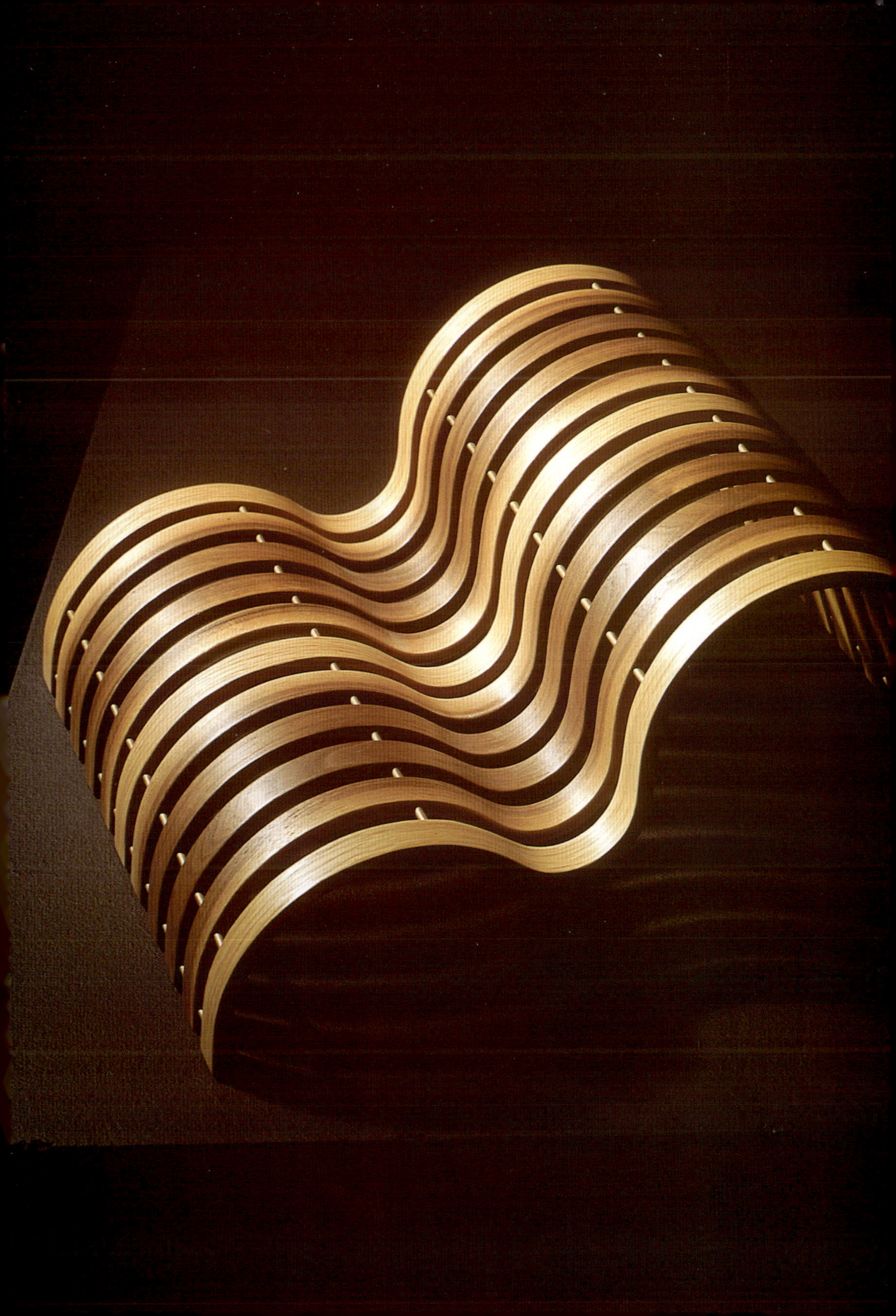

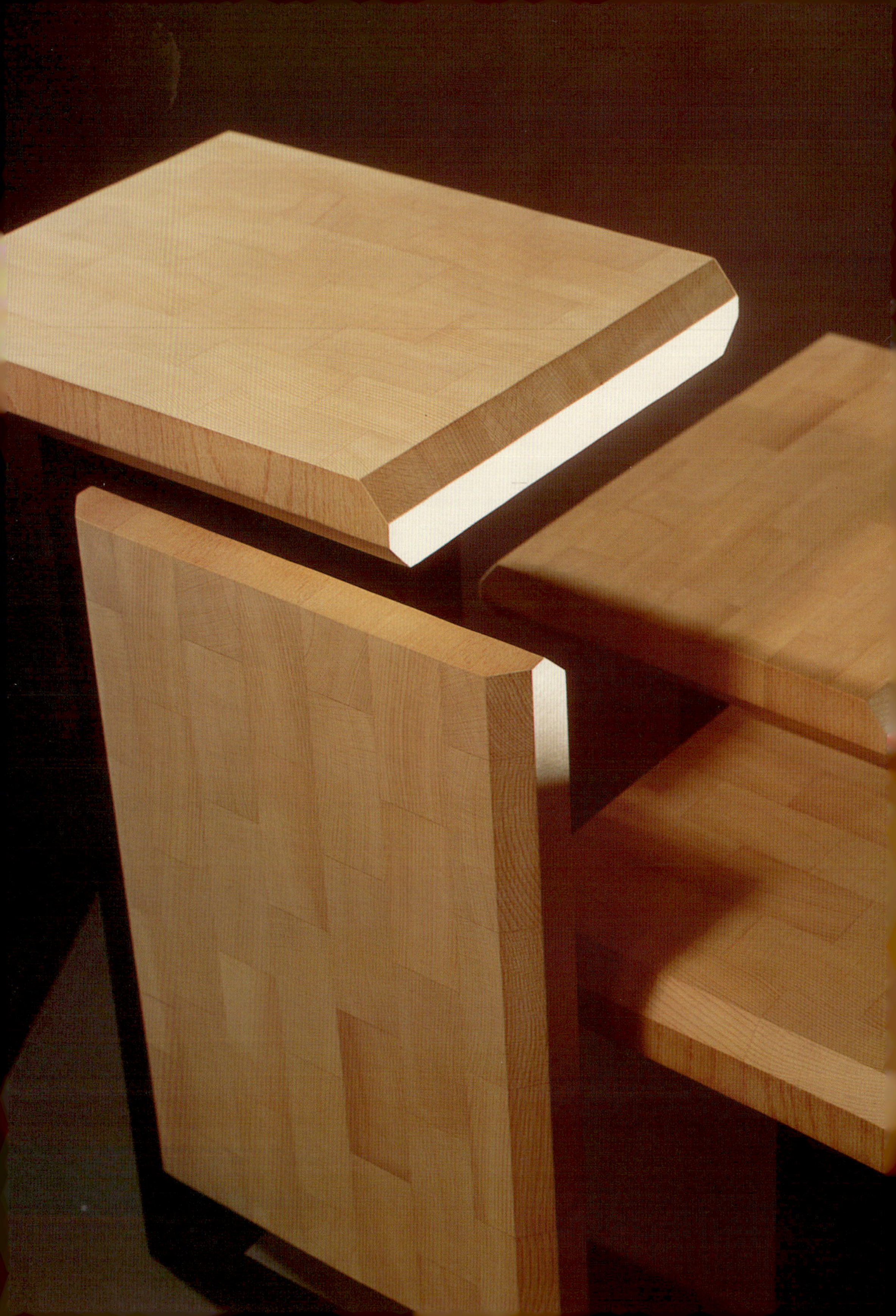

←Jeremy Madden
Butcher's Block
Steamed beech
40 x 36 x 28
Batch Production Project
FP1

Conceived from personal necessity the form of this butcher's block is adaptable to any kitchen environment. The terseness of the beech enabled the end grain to be manipulated into a rectangled pattern and also renders it more resistant to knife strokes. The chamfered ends provide a grip for fingers.

↑Brian Murray
Rock Drawers
Maple and walnut
14.5 x 7 x 6
Client Commission
Graduate

These memory drawer boxes are intended for triplets. Each box is eventually to contain a baby's cherished first lock of hair, or a toddler's first tooth. The disparate use of woods and the intuitiveness of the form reflect the designer's discerning vision.

FURNISHING THE DETAILS | 47

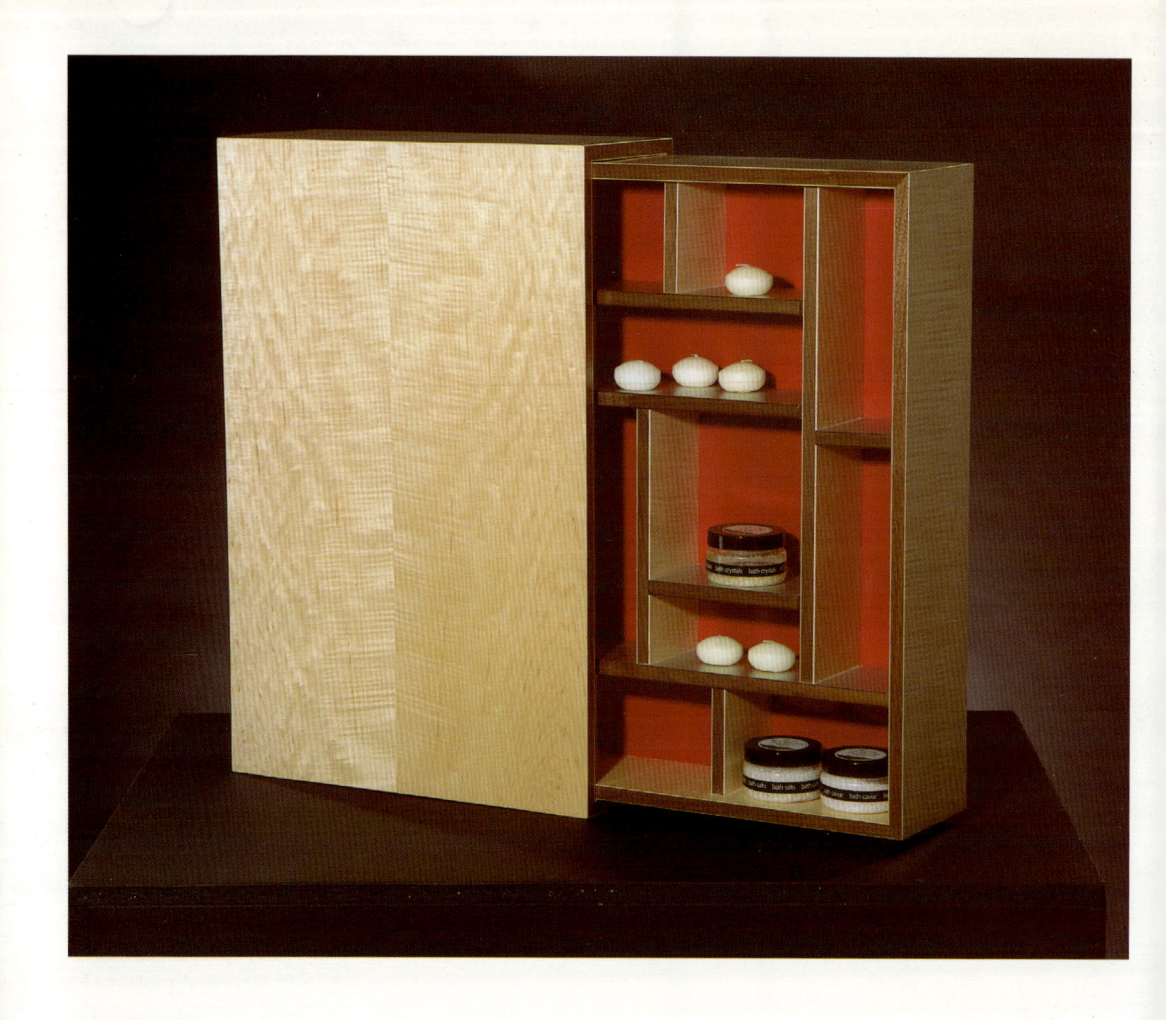

↑ Diarmuid Murphy
Bathroom Storage Cabinet
Maple, MDF, walnut, brushed steel laminate and PC lacquer
59.5 x 40 x 17
Innovative Bathroom Furniture Project
FDM2
This bathroom cabinet is quite architectonic in design. The central door encloses an asymmetrical storage system which can hold a variety of personal ephemera. The reflective qualities of the materials and the brushed steel laminate add to the overall sense of light and sophistication.

→ Nigel Paxton
Seat and Storage Unit
Oak and Danish oil
72 x 42 x 30
Innovative Bathroom Furniture Project
FDM2
The Bauhaus philosophy of functionalism was the inspiration behind this multifunctional piece of furniture. The constructional principles of this dual seat storage unit create an innovative, contemporary piece of furniture suitable to any modern environment.

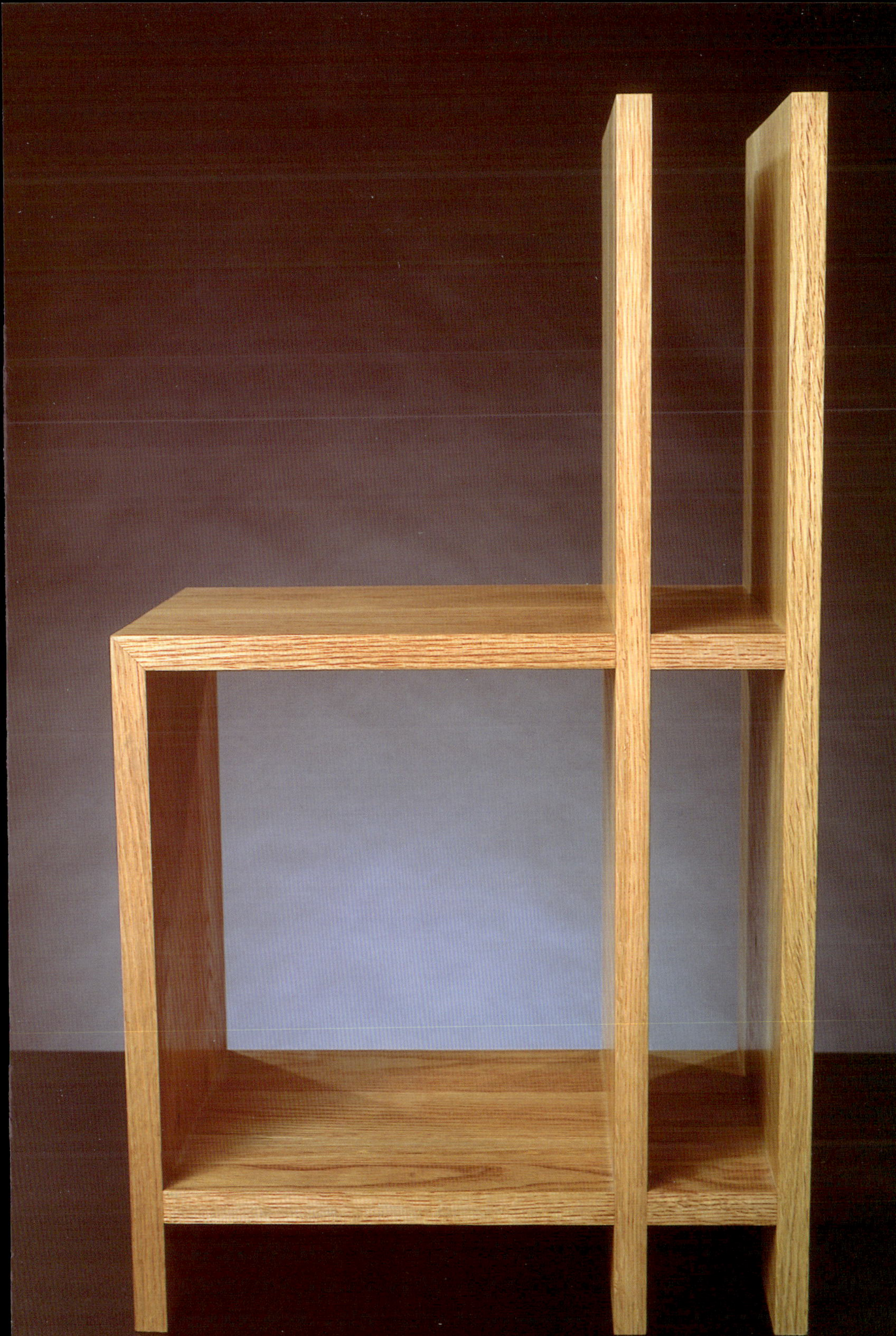

50 FURNISHING THE DETAILS

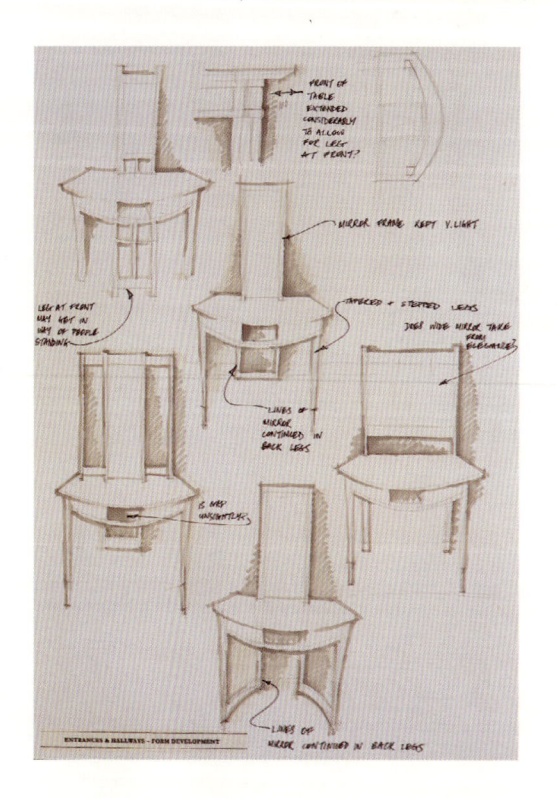

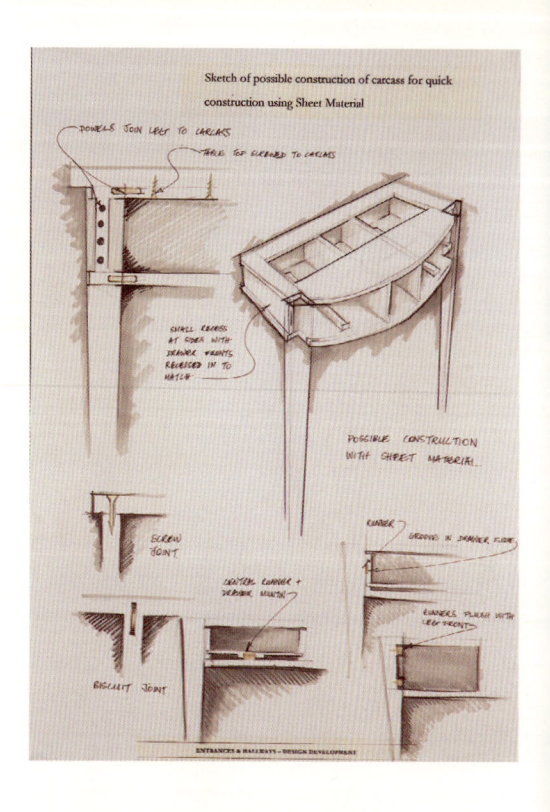

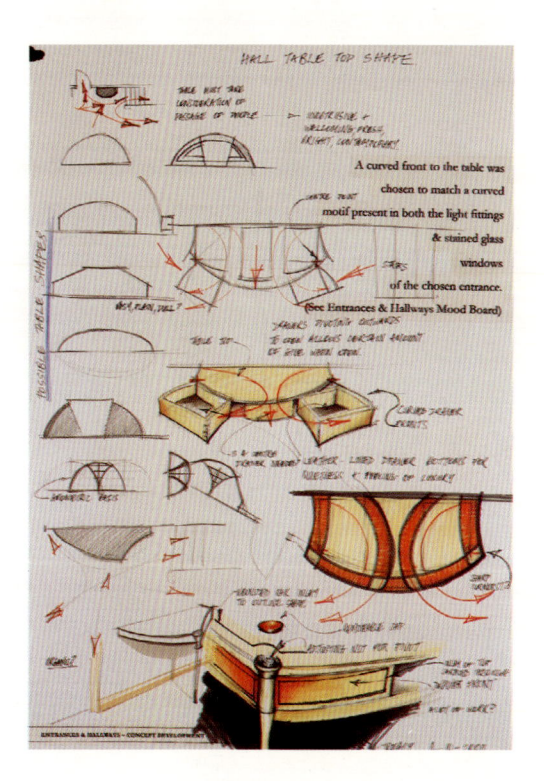

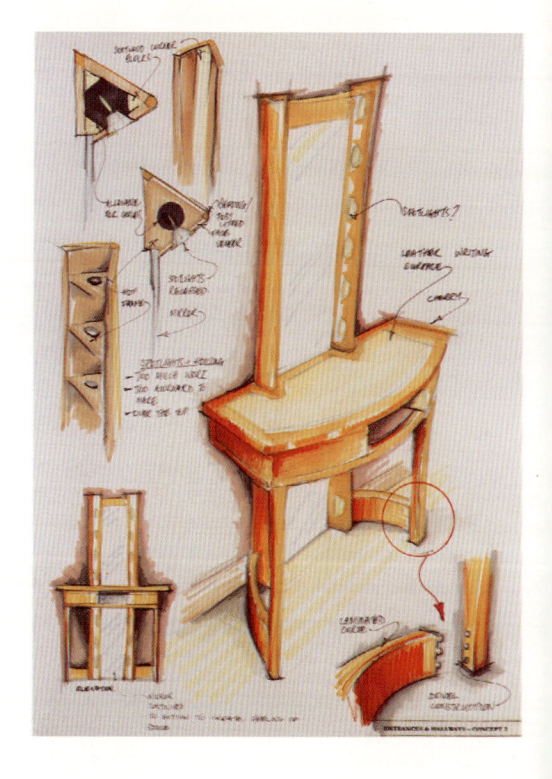

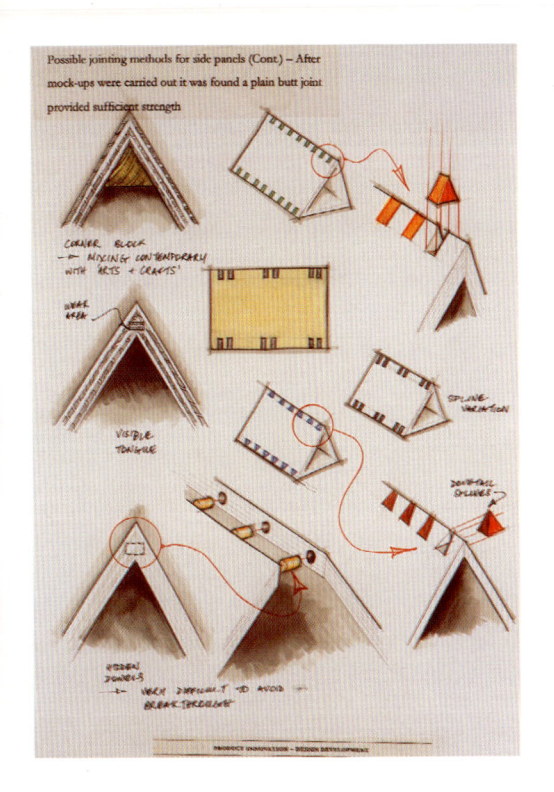

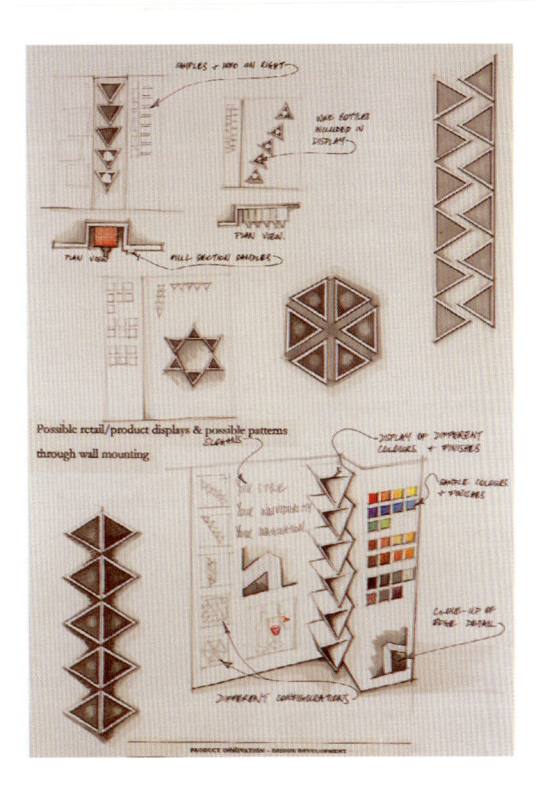

←Alan Treacy
Hallstand
Entrances and Hallways Project
Graduate

This hallstand was designed for a modern family home. Initially the form was in contrast to its surroundings. As the design progressed it was paired down to its essentials, both functionally and aesthetically, resulting in a classical piece with a contemporary twist.

↑Alan Treacy
Wine Rack
Innovation Project
Graduate

These design exploration drawings demonstrate constructional considerations and analysis of form and pattern, in the development of a storage system for wine bottles. The concept involves a single storage unit which can be stacked or wall mounted in an array of shapes and arrangements, which are based on repetition of form/units, thus allowing individuality for the end user.

A PERSPECTIVE

Ireland's design history is a controversial one, marred by long periods when few industries recognised the commercial importance of good design. Factories did not have trained designers; rather designs were copied from neighbouring countries. Generally there existed a poor critique of good design in the country. Furthermore consumers did not have disposable income. Since its opening in 1987, GMIT Letterfrack Furniture College has left an indelible mark on Irish design. Its pioneering workshops, original courses, degree programmes and innovative teaching techniques have attracted many talented designers, craftspeople and technologists to its doors. The College's accomplishments in various fields have created a symbiotic rapport between national and international design related industries, producing a standard of work that is unique.

The village of Letterfrack is located in a sparse landscape at the heart of rugged Connemara. To some, the isolation of the College is key in stimulating a hegemonic environment, where national and international crafts people and designers may concentrate solely on design and manufacture. Without a doubt its geographical position has provided the impetus for an innovative and creative vision that has permeated its way into our national heritage.

The building where the College is housed has become a metaphor for this vision, as it successfully marries the old and the new. GMIT Letterfrack is the only Institute in Ireland offering students a range of degree programmes in furniture design, manufacture, production and technology, conservation and restoration[1]. The differentiation between the diverse disciplines on offer at the College is important and is key to its recipe for success. The B. Sc. in Furniture Design and Manufacture course balances that mystical mixture between design, fabrication and technology. Using creative techniques and a wide range of skills one can design and make innovative prototypes and original furniture. One can witness the rewarding evolution of creating a concept, making the prototype and watching it flourish into its final form.

From there one progresses to the B. Sc. in Product Design (Furniture) course, which teaches advanced skills in furniture design using high-end CAD/CAM systems, industrial design and prototyping techniques. The B. Sc. in Furniture Production and Technology course is all about methodology. It embraces analytical thinking, emphasising a completely different speciality within the design field. Production here is the principal focus, where one plans, efficiently organises and implements the precise construction of high quality furniture. Through the use of current furniture manufacturing technologies and state of the art production systems one develops the skill, knowledge and competence of machine use. By further undertaking the B. Sc. in Manufacturing Technology (Furniture) course an advanced skill in manufacturing, using computer-controlled technology is acquired.

Future education is pivotal in understanding and appreciating design, graphics and furniture making. This is addressed at GMIT Letterfrack by the B. Sc. in Design and Technology Education course. Woodworking, designing and making furniture is linked with a theoretical understanding of education, teaching skills and

A PERSPECTIVE (contd)

classroom techniques. Graduates from this program can actively engage Junior and Leaving Certificate students through a plethora of construction principles, architectural and furniture technology, design, communication and technical graphics. This provides a strong foundation to future generations encouraging them to develop and express their creativity.

Conservation and restoration is also fundamentally important in creating insight into furniture and wooden objects used by past generations. The B.Sc. in Furniture Conservation and Restoration course shows conservators how to treat historic objects, with the aim of preserving and restoring their original function, appearance and value. Through applying science, microscopic analysis and photography combined with skills in traditional woodworking and the use of modern machines students learn about the history of furniture and various stylistic movements.

The legacy of GMIT at Letterfrack is the way in which the various courses address relevant issues in design, both past and present. Since it opened its workshops have provided the highest quality education and training, giving graduates lifelong transferable skills and abilities which they can put into practice anywhere in the world.

Jennifer Goff, B.A., M.A., Art & Design Historian

July 2006

1 The GMIT Letterfrack campus currently offers six B. Sc. programmes as follows:

B.Sc. in Furniture Design and Manufacture
B.Sc. in Furniture Production and Technology
B.Sc. in Furniture Conservation and Restoration
B.Sc. (Hons) in Design and Technology Education
B.Sc. (Hons) in Manufacturing Technology {Furniture}
B. Sc. (Hons) in Product Design {Furniture}

LISTING OF EXHIBITS ON SHOW BUT NOT FEATURED IN THE CATALOGUE

3. Colin Cannon
Coffee Table
MDF with walnut lippings and veneers
40 x 190 x 45
21st Century Project, FDM2
The expressive qualities of the materials used in this coffee table enhance its modern appeal, making it pertinent to the project brief which stipulated that the piece be relevant in one hundred years time. The geometric structure is unconventional through the mixture of solid and open square shapes.

9. Peter Drumm
Sink Unit
American maple with waterproof finish
21 x 71 x 44
Innovative Bathroom Furniture Project, FDM2
Inspired by the crisp clean lines of the simple modernist forms of the early twentieth century, this sink unit is timeless in its style and rationale. Manifesting a structural and functional ideology, the sensitive use of materials would befit any contemporary bathroom.

22. David Duffy
Wine Rack
Birch plywood and paint
41 x 57.5 x 23
CNC Project, FP2
This inventive birch plywood wine rack is simple yet also functional. The unctuous forms of the curved frame can be extended through the addition of more racks. The intense colour and the use of mild steel inserts transform what is a basic utility object into a desirable household item.

29. Andrew Stephenson and Peter Ranalow
Desk Tidy, Pencil Holder
Cherry, ash, laminated constructional veneer and plywood veneer
45 x 28 x 8
Corporate Gift Project, FP2 and FDM2
This sleek pencil holder is composed of two pieces of curved wood. Constructed from either cherry or ash it terminates in a neat rectangle repository for desk objects, writing paraphernalia and other stationery items. Due to its functional design a batch of thirty was created.

33. Gearóid Donohoe
Mirror – Infinity
Wenge and maple
66 x 46
Design and Make - Final Project, FDM1
This mirror suggests a person's outward appearance which is a reflection and representation of the inner person. The crisp decoration of the mirror with its dark lines and red edging encapsulates an aesthetic idea, framing and adding support to the piece through the patterns it creates.

39. Paul Leamy
Folding Seat
Sweet chestnut
60.8 x 28.8 x 23.8
Design and Make Project, Graduate, Staff
This folding seat was inspired by sitting umbrellas. Made from sweet chestnut, it is flexible in form and combines an interest in efficient furniture design with structural ingenuity. It reveals an avid interest in traditional materials and sensitivity for the natural qualities and organic properties of the wood.

41. Peter Ranalow
Curved Bathroom Drawer
Birch plywood with matt black finish
13.5 x 50 x 15
Innovative Bathroom Furniture Project, FDM2
This piece is designed to be both functional and visually stimulating. The versatile design demonstrates its ability to be used in a variety of different environments. A strong tonal and colour contrast, achieved by the use of the matt finish, underlines its effortless style.

42. Alastair Creswell
Marquetry Panel
Pear, sycamore and padouk
24 x 12
Marquetry Project, FDM2
The panel illustrates water being collected into an amphora. The scroll represents time being peeled back. Pear wood was used due to its wrinkled properties, symbolising rippling water. Sycamore was employed for its plainer qualities. Padauk, with its dark reddish straight lines, denotes the depth and richness of history.

43. David Carpendale
Bath Salts Dispenser
Hand carved lime with aluminium supporting base and mechanism
27 x 10 x 7.5
Innovative Bathroom Furniture Project, FDM2
Entitled *Neptune* this innovative range of bath salts dispensers was inspired by the enduring history of Roman bath culture. Environmentally aware, its aim is to eliminate the distribution and use of plastic bottles in the bathroom. Its humanist qualities aspire to stimulate the senses and induce relaxation.

44. Niall Galligan
Mini Walnut Cube
Walnut
6 x 6 x 6
CNC Project, FP2
The project brief for this minimalist cube was to demonstrate knowledge of CNC. The end product is an observance in mathematical precision and accuracy. Walnut was chosen for its suitability in exemplifying the grained pattern. The form was spray finished which reveals the lustrous colour of the wood.

45. Alan Melbourne, Michael Langtry and John Scanlan
Oak and Walnut Shelves
Oak and walnut
62 x 43 x 15
Skills Development Project, FP1
Created from a working drawing this shelving system is composed of oak and walnut parts. After veneering the pieces and routing the rounded edges the shelves were assembled. Oak and walnut provide a visual contrast. Finished with a pre-catalysed lacquer, its soft qualities reflect the woods' patina.

47. Thomas Flaherty
Mudejar Style Table
Walnut, poplar, ebony, boxwood, mother of pearl and bone
36 x 28 x 24
Conservation Project, FCR2
Dating from the late 19th early 20th century the complexities of this table provided a conservation challenge. The inlay required sensitive consolidation using hot protein glue. With the lacunae replaced and the lost surface coating reinstated, this table adroitly demonstrates the Mudejar style.

48. Eamonn Cunningham
Súgán Chair
Ash and súgán
87 x 53 x 43
Conservation Project, FCR2
The frame of this lack lustre, mistreated chair had been badly damaged by caustic soda. With an appreciation of the súgán tradition, which refers to the straw rope seating, this chair was lovingly conserved and restored using the traditional twisting and weaving methodology.

49. Maurice O'Sullivan and Ruaidhrí O Bolguidhir
Folding Demi Lune Table
Mahogany, satinwood, tulipwood and brass
73 x 91 x 45
Conservation Project, Graduate and FCR3
This Georgian table required structural consolidation. Its knuckle joint mechanism and leg joints necessitated attention. Missing straight and herring bone patterned banding was replaced. Warping had caused structural and aesthetic problems. By removing the surface coating and sensitively retouching, the splendour of this table is evident again.

50. Henning Schulze
Single Row Spindle Back Side Chair
Ash and elm
83 x 48 x 36
Conservation Project, Staff
Dating between 1820 and 1860, the chair's original function had to be reinstated. Conversion into a rocking chair and loss of the rocking rails required replacing front leg sections in excentric turning. The shrunken seat had fallen out of the frame, requiring attention. Maintaining its worn look, this piece retains its character.

51. Frances Clohessy
Desk Tidy and Pen Holder
Beech, walnut and oak
12 x 10 x 8
Batch Production Project, FP1
This small, understated piece provided an interesting challenge. After waxing, assembling and gluing the inside, a two millimetre fillet was put on the edges. After sanding, it was coated with bees wax and buffed with sheep's wool. The combination of woods gives the piece visual finesse and a superior finish.

52. Liam McDonagh
Nest of Tables
MDF sprayed with high gloss and glass top
45 x 45 x 45
Contemporary Living Project, B.Sc. 4
This is a refreshing slant on the classic nest of tables. The geometric shape and use of a contrasting black and white colour scheme are directly inspired by current fashion trends. These four tables can also be used as seating.

53. Gavin O'Kelly
Keepsake Box
Maple, Macassar ebony, sycamore and spalted beech interior
26.7 x 16.5 x 10
Design and Make Project, Graduate
Bearing emotional significance this box houses keepsakes from the infancy of the designer's children. It is an expression of interdependent dualities. The linear, ordered outside represents reason, whilst the unfettered inside evokes romantic undertones. Asymmetrical dovetail features complement the random beech markings.

54. John Lee
Carraig - Chest of Drawers
White Oak
85 x 160 x 60
Gallery Piece, Graduate
The sculptural forms of this chest of drawers were directly inspired by the Connemara landscape. Its sweeping lines unite its structural finesse and dynamism. Its distinct qualities emphasise its elegant appearance, yet it remains eminently practical.

55. Laura Mays
Chairs
Maple and hornbeam
90 x 45 x 45
Gallery Piece, Graduate
Through the employment of two exceedingly white woods, maple and hornbeam, this design maintains a floating, insouciant effect. Their composition reveals an aerodynamic ideology which combines with the lines to produce a raffish, unusual design.

56. Brian Murray
Container
Padouk, steamed beech and ebony
155 x 38 x 27
Client Commission, Graduate
This piece contains a secret compartment. It is the perfect repository for storing important and personal documents such as passports, birth certificates, treasured correspondence, etc. This tall, thin yet stable cabinet maintains a sculptural quality and practicality.

57. Brian Murray
Dining Table with Four Chairs
Native walnut and birdseye maple
106 x 142 x 75
Client Commission, Graduate
This circular table is accompanied by four sculpted walnut chairs. The backs of the chairs have an hour glass figure. This forms a major part of their aesthetic appeal. They are normally viewed from a rear perspective.

58. Jonathan Madden
Photographer's Meeting Table
Burr oak, rippled sycamore, walnut and glass
90 x 45
Client Commission, Graduate
This individual piece was commissioned by one of Ireland's leading wedding photographers. The form of the meeting table was designed to create a space so that photograph albums could be stored in a unique fashion, whilst still being readily accessible to present to potential clients.

59. Jonathan Madden
Dining Suite
Ash and burr oak
250 x 110 x 73 (table), 50 x 46 x various heights (chairs)
Client Commission, Graduate
The aim was to create and produce an elegant and functional cohesive suite – literally and visually. The dimensions of the chairs and the stylish lines of the table purposefully engage one another. The subtle variation in the design of each of the chairs complements the central theme of the collection.

60. Thomas Duggan
Storage Chest
Cherrywood
82 x 140 x 75
Client Commission, Graduate

design: www.vermilliondesign.com

For further information on courses at the college or designers featured in this exhibition catalogue please contact

letterfrack@gmit.ie

or write to

Sanchia O'Connor
GMIT at Letterfrack
Letterfrack,
Co. Galway.
Ireland

Tel: 095 41660
Fax: 095 41112